Fact.

The giraffe was originally called a "cameleopard" because fourteenth-century Romans thought the animal looked like a cross between a camel and a leopard.

Fact.

Giraffes need a serious ticker to get blood up those long necks to their brains: A giraffe heart often weighs up to 25 pounds, and can be more than 2 feet long.

LEARN THE TRUTH AND SPOT THE LIE

**on Everything from Tequila-Made Diamonds to *Tetris*'s Soviet Roots—
Plus Tons of Other Totally Random Facts from Science, History, and Beyond!**

Bullsh*t!

Giraffes are one of the sleepiest mammals around; they average a whopping fifteen hours of sleep per twenty-four-hour period. They're great at hiding it, however: They only sleep standing up.

Neil Patrick Stewart

Published by
Adams Media, a division of F+W Media, Inc.
57 Littlefield Street, Avon, MA 02322. U.S.A.
www.adamsmedia.com

ISBN 10: 1-4405-2553-6
ISBN 13: 978-1-4405-2553-7
eISBN 10: 1-4405-2775-X
eISBN 13: 978-1-4405-2775-3

Printed in the United States of America.

10 9 8 7 6 5 4 3

Library of Congress Cataloging-in-Publication Data
is available from the publisher.

This publication is designed to provide accurate and authoritative information with regard to the subject matter covered. It is sold with the understanding that the publisher is not engaged in rendering legal, accounting, or other professional advice. If legal advice or other expert assistance is required, the services of a competent professional person should be sought.
—From a *Declaration of Principles* jointly adopted by a Committee of the American Bar Association and a Committee of Publishers and Associations

Many of the designations used by manufacturers and sellers to distinguish their product are claimed as trademarks. Where those designations appear in this book and Adams Media was aware of a trademark claim, the designations have been printed with initial capital letters.

Line art © 2011 clipart.com
Sillhouettes © Neubau Welt

*This book is available at quantity discounts for bulk purchases.
For information, please call 1-800-289-0963.*

CONTENTS

Introduction: How Good Is Your Bullshit Detector? **vi**

CHAPTER 1

Kingdom Animalia 1

The Giraffe! 3
The Dog! 5
The Falcon! 7
The Duck-Billed Platypus! 9
The Frog! 11
The Skunk! 13
The Cockroach! 15
The Baboon! 17
The Hummingbird! 19
The Panda! 21
The Cow! 23
The Squirrel! 25
The Earthworm! 27
The Snow Leopard! 29
The Elephant! 31
The Manatee! 33
The Tyrannosaurus! 35
The Swan! 37
The Otter! 39
The Shark! 41
The Koala! 43
The Liger! 45
The Unicorn! 47

CHAPTER 2

Pop Culture! 49

Back to the Future! 51
The Cell Phone! 53
Rubik's Cube! 55
The Beatles! 57
Soap Operas! 59
Barbie! 61
Jeans! 63
Star Wars! 65
Star Trek! 67
Tetris! 69
Zombies! 71
Monopoly! 73
Oprah! 75
Dungeons & Dragons! 77
The Wedgie! 79
Harry Potter! 81
LOL! 83
YouTube! 85
Bugs Bunny! 87
The Moustache! 89
Superman! 91
Supercalifragilisticexpialidocious! 93
The iPod! 95
Jazz! 97

CHAPTER 3

Everything Edible 99

Coca-Cola! **101**
The Tomato! **103**
Rice! **105**
French Fries! **107**
Marshmallows! **109**
Beer! **111**
Sliced Bread! **113**
High-Fructose Corn Syrup! **115**
Bacon! **117**
Pepper! **119**
Watermelon! **121**
Cheese! **123**
The Sandwich! **125**
Tequila! **127**
Jell-O! **129**
Chocolate! **131**
The Hot Dog! **133**
The Ice Cream Sundae! **135**
The Apple! **137**
The Fortune Cookie! **139**
Honey! **141**
Gummi Bears! **143**
The Twinkie! **145**
Spam! **147**

CHAPTER 4

Famous Dead People 149

Elvis! **151**
Harry Houdini! **153**
Helen Keller! **155**
Marie Curie! **157**
Michael Jackson! **159**

The Elephant Man! **161**
Picasso! **163**
Jimi Hendrix! **165**
William Shakespeare! **167**
Al Capone! **169**
Martin Luther King, Jr.! **171**
Albert Einstein! **173**
Confucius! **175**
Ronald Reagan! **177**
Che Guevara! **179**
Napoleon! **181**
Anne Frank! **183**
Walt Disney! **185**
Marilyn Monroe! **187**
Thomas Jefferson! **189**
Cleopatra! **191**
Mozart! **193**
Amelia Earhart! **195**
Gandhi! **197**
Boring! **199**

CHAPTER 5

Weird Science 201

The Sun! **203**
Plastic Surgery! **205**
Life! **207**
Gold! **209**
Cloning! **211**
Pi! **213**
Pee! **215**
P! **217**
Electrocution! **219**
The Robot! **221**
Dentistry! **223**
Bacteria! **225**

Fact. Fact. **Bullsh*t!**

Fingernails! 227
Lasers! 229
Hiccups! 231
Viagra! 233
The Milky Way! 235
Mind Control! 237
Pregnancy! 239
Flamethrowers! 241
The Atom! 243
Magnets! 245
Blood! 247
Uranus! 249

CHAPTER 6
Sports and Other Wastes of Time 251

The Football! 253
Jousting! 255
The NBA! 257
Volleyball! 259
Luge! 261
Archery! 263
The Yo-Yo! 265
The Frisbee! 267
Lucha Libre! 269
Nascar! 271
Cluster Ballooning! 273
The Baseball Glove! 275
Ice Skating! 277
Tug of War! 279
Synchronized Swimming! 281
Karate! 283
The Jockstrap! 285
The Sports Bra! 287

The Cleveland Indians! 289
Ping-Pong! 291
Weightlifting! 293
Pillow Fighting! 295
Strange Sports! 297

CHAPTER 7
Florilegium, Omnium-Gatherum, and Gallimaufry 299

The Toothbrush! 301
Bank Robbery! 303
Toilet Paper! 305
Stonehenge! 307
Valentine's Day! 309
New Jersey! 311
Severed Feet! 313
The White House! 315
Holy Cow!!! 317
1950! 319
Hugs! 321
Impostors! 323
Rare Books! 325
Pajamas! 327
Eleven! 329
Murder! 331
Tuesday! 333
Pink! 335
The Pencil! 337
Feline Cruelty! 339
Exploding Whales! 341
Laughter! 343

INTRODUCTION
HOW GOOD IS YOUR BULLSHIT DETECTOR?

Everyone's an expert. As kids, we breathlessly informed each other that swallowed chewing gum takes seven years to digest. My best friend likes to point out that we need eight glasses of water a day to be healthy. My uncle taught me that the alcohol burns away when you cook with wine, and a pet store cashier recently remarked to me that goldfish have a memory span of just a few seconds. A barber once instructed me that shaving causes hair to grow back even thicker, and a college classmate smugly pointed out to a group of us that glass is actually a liquid that moves very, very slowly. A tour guide once told the group that water drains out of a toilet according to the Coriolis effect, and a particular public speaker seemed to be looking at me when she said that men think about sex every seven seconds.

All of these things, however, are bullshit. Conventional wisdom is quite often not wisdom at all, just a series of old wives' tales that we repeat to each other endlessly in a brainless worldwide game of Bullshit Telephone. I've always thought people are capable of believing just about anything they hear, and I intend to prove it. I bet I can make up complete fabrications about topics you're familiar with, and that you'll buy it—hook, line, and sinker. At least, some of the time you will.

Care to prove me wrong? I've collected a mountain of data on a plethora of topics, ranging from Elvis Presley to the duck-billed platypus, added a healthy dose of bullshit to the mix, then stirred it all up.

On every page, you'll find three statements about a particular topic, of which *two are true and one is a lie*. Make your call, then turn the page to find out if you're right. My wager is that more often than not, you'll be surprised at what you find.

Fact. Fact. **Bullsh*t!**

CHAPTER 1

Kingdom Animalia

Currently, there are about 2 million species on the planet (that we know about), and scientists figure there are probably at least twice that many—perhaps even fifteen times that many—living and dying around us every day. Any biologist worth her salt will tell you that she's learned enough to know just how much she *doesn't know* about animals. Which is a lot.

We do know enough, however, to help preserve endangered species, to improve a sick or injured animal's condition, and to take excellent care of our pets. We ought to know something: We humans are animals too.

But we're more than just animals, right? We have culture, language, tools, personality, emotions, and morals, after all. That makes us something more. That's what makes us *human*.

Bullshit. Different species of animals have been proven to possess each one of those things, in turn, and scientists continue to be surprised on a regular basis by what animals turn out to be capable of accomplishing.

If you doubt the fact that you know far fewer things about animals than you think you do, turn the page, spot the bullshit, and prove me wrong.

Fact. Fact. **Bullsh*t!**

THE GIRAFFE!

1. Lugging around that long neck is tiring! Giraffes are one of the sleepiest mammals around; they average a whopping fifteen hours of sleep per twenty-four-hour period. They're great at hiding it, however: They only sleep standing up.

---

2. The giraffe was originally called a "cameleopard." Fourteenth-century Romans came up with the name because they thought the beast looked like a cross between a camel and a leopard. The Afrikaans language still takes its cues from the Romans, calling the giraffe the *kameelperd*.

---

3. Giraffes need a serious ticker to get blood up those long necks to their brains: A giraffe heart often weighs up to 25 pounds, and can be more than 2 feet long.

1. **Bullshit!** In fact, the **opposite** is true. Giraffes need less sleep than most other mammals, and sometimes they sleep as little as ten minutes in a given day. On average, they sleep between thirty to 120 minutes daily. While they can sleep standing up, they also curl up on the ground and sleep with their head resting on their own rump. Giraffes often doze in very short bursts, keeping their ears perked to listen for predators.

2. **Fact.** Those silly Romans! Have you ever seen a camel or a leopard with a 6-foot neck?

3. **Fact.** Giraffe hearts have special valves to regulate blood pressure, depending on whether the head is raised (eating from a tree) or lowered (drinking from a spring). Without its specialized heart, raising its head would lead to such a drastic change in blood pressure that the giraffe would faint.

Fact. Fact. **Bullsh*t!**

THE DOG!

1. The dog is the most widely kept companion animal in human history. There is approximately one dog for every seventeen people on Earth. In the United States, we have dog fever: There is one dog for every four people.

---

2. The fox is actually a kind of dog. Domesticated silver foxes that behave just like normal dogs were bred in painstaking selective-breeding experiments that were begun sixty years ago by Soviet scientists.

---

3. A dog's sense of smell is so well developed that it can perceive odors at concentrations sixty times lower than a human can.

1. **Fact.** It is estimated that there are 400 million dogs on the planet, and 6.77 billion people. That's one dog for every 16.9425 people. We'll call that seventeen. Roughly 308 million people live in the U.S., and approximately 77.5 million dogs. That's one dog for every 3.9742 people. We'll call it four.

   While cats are more popular than dogs in the U.S (one cat for every 3.3 people), dogs have been domesticated by humans for more than 12,000 years (some experts put it closer to 100,000), whereas cats became domesticated roughly 5,000 years ago. (It's up for debate as to whether cats are domesticated at all.)

   ---

2. **Fact.** The project was set up in 1959 by Soviet scientist Dmitri Belyaev. The foxes were selected based on tame behavior for over forty generations, and the project produced foxes that are extremely friendly towards humans, wag their tails, and like to lick faces.

   The term "dog" can be used to refer to any member of the family Canidae. Under this definition, foxes, wolves, jackals, and dingoes are all dogs. The prairie dog is not, in fact, a dog. (Neither is the dogfish.)

3. **Bullsh*t!** The dog's ability to smell should be considered a superpower. Dogs can perceive odors at concentrations nearly **100 million** times lower than a human.

   Your dog's icky wet nose also aids its sense of smell: The wetness helps it determine the direction of the air current, which in turn helps it determine the direction a smell is coming from.

THE FALCON!

1. Peregrine falcons are exceedingly rare and critically endangered, with numerous conservation efforts in full swing to keep them around. Hampering progress is the fact that peregrines are among the slowest-moving birds of prey, and are consistently outperformed in their habitat.

2. All kestrels (such as the Madagascar kestrel and the gray kestrel), hobbies (such as the African hobby and the Oriental hobby), and merlins (such as the black merlin and the prairie merlin) are falcons. All falcons (such as the red-necked falcon and the bat falcon) are raptors. Eagles, hawks, and vultures are also raptors.

3. A groundbreaking gene study published in 2008 suggests that falcons are actually more closely related to parrots than to hawks or eagles.

1. **Bullsh*t!** Peregrine falcons are neither rare nor endangered. On the contrary, they can be found nearly everywhere on the planet, from the highest mountains to the densest tropics. They are the most widespread bird of prey.

   They are also hands-down the **fastest animal in the world**, having been clocked at **240 miles per hour** during a dive.

2. **Fact.** The term "raptor" loosely refers to birds of prey that hunt during the day, whereas birds of prey that hunt at night are called owls.

   Kestrels, hobbies, and merlins are all members of the genus *Falco* and the order Falconiformes, making them falcons.

---

3. **Fact.** The finding, sponsored by the National Science Foundation's "Assembling the Tree of Life" initiative, is counter to the assumptions made by ornithologists for decades. If proven to be true, falcons may wind up getting evicted from the order Falconiformes, which was, obviously, named after them.

   That would be like kicking Dave Matthews out of the Dave Matthews Band.

THE DUCK-BILLED PLATYPUS!

1. The platypus was first discovered by European explorers in 1849, and early British settlers in Australia (its native environment) called it a beaverduck. The plural of platypus is "platypi."

---

2. Besides being one of just a few species of mammals that lay eggs, the platypus is one of a very few species of mammals that are actually venomous! A male platypus has a spur above the foot in each hind leg that can inject poison produced by a gland in its thigh.

---

3. A mother platypus will nurse her young, but not with help from her nipples: She doesn't have any. Instead milk is secreted through pores in her abdomen, which the babies scrape up with their bills.

1. **Bullsh*t!** European explorers discovered the animal in 1798, and British settlers commonly referred to the platypus by many names, including the **watermole**, **duckbill**, and **duckmole**, but not beaverduck. While colloquially used, "platypi" is not a correct pluralized form of platypus.

    There is no universally agreed-upon plural form, since both "platypus" and "platypuses" are thought to be correct in different circles.

2. **Fact.** The spur is about 15 millimeters long, and a platypus will use it to defend itself. The gland in the thigh is called the crural gland. While not deadly to humans, the venom can cause quite a bit of discomfort. The best way to pick up a platypus and not get poisoned is by the tip of the tail.

    Other venomous mammals are the Eurasian water shrew and the European mole.

3. **Fact.** While she does have mammary glands, a female platypus has no teats. It's a good thing too—a baby platypus is born with a full set of teeth. The teeth fall out after a couple of weeks.

THE FROG!

1. Many people get frogs and toads confused, but they are in fact two completely separate taxonomic groups, from different orders and families. The resemblance between the two is a biological marvel, since one has to go way back on the evolutionary timeline to find a common ancestor.

2. Frogs of the genus *Ceratophrys* are known as pacman frogs, because of their huge mouths and round shape, as well as their tendency to try to swallow anything that they can fit their prodigious mouths around, including fish, mice, lizards, and even birds.

3. Frogs are biological wonders: They have no external ears, a great many are able to breathe and drink through their skin, and most frogs actually have teeth.

1. **Bullsh*t!** Taxonomy makes no distinction between frogs and toads. In fact, contrary to widely held belief, **all toads are frogs**. This explains why they resemble one another so closely! All frogs and toads are amphibians of the order Anura, and many species of frog and toad come from the same family.

2. **Fact.** A pacman frog will sometimes even try to swallow things it *can't* get its mouth around, such as rodents twice its size. Unfortunately, this practice typically causes the frog to suffocate and die. Such frogs are fearless and some will actually leap at and attack anything that threatens them, even if vastly overmatched, such as a human.

   Pacman frogs will even try to swallow other pacman frogs, including their mates. For this reason, pet stores helpfully suggest you keep them in separate tanks.

3. **Fact.** Rather than ears, frogs have tympanums, a structure similar to a drumhead. Frogs do have inner ears.

   Frog skin is water-permeable, which means water can be absorbed through the skin. Many frogs absorb oxygen in the same way. The permeable skin does leave frogs vulnerable to drying out, which is why we often observe frogs crouching in water.

   Most frogs actually do have teeth, generally in the form of one row of upper teeth, or maxillary teeth. They often have teeth further back on the roof of their mouths as well, or vomerine teeth. Frogs never have lower teeth. The teeth aren't used to chew—frogs generally swallow their food whole.

THE SKUNK!

1. Keeping skunks as pets is illegal in many states, and in all of Canada. Still, there is a major underground movement advocating the little stinkers as excellent companion animals. Much like declawing, pet skunks are routinely de-scented by a veterinarian-performed surgical procedure.

2. The word "skunk" comes from the Algonquian word *segonku*, which literally means "one who squirts." The German word for skunk is *Stinktier*.

3. The skunk's powerful scent is emitted from a single small gland at the base of the tail. The skunk only has enough juice for one healthy spray before it needs to "recharge," but it is a doozy: It can spray up to 9 feet!

1. **Fact.** Once the scent gland is removed, skunks make excellent pets. Domesticated skunks are intelligent, curious, and can be very loving and cuddly. At press time, about 30 percent of states allow skunk ownership. There are many activists in other states and Canada pressing for legalization.

Some qualified vets can perform an operation to remove the scent gland. In the U.K., owning skunks as pets is perfectly legal, but the operation is not, making the idea thoroughly impractical. (Unless you have no sense of smell and hate houseguests.)

---

2. **Fact.** "Skunk" is a corruption of the Abenaki word *segonku* or *segongw*. The Abenaki people are a subdivision of the Algonquian nation.

3. **Bullsh*t!** The skunk has two **anal** scent glands, one on either side. The skunk can blast a full spray **five or six times** before it needs to let the chemicals build up again, which can take over a week. The skunk can spray with great accuracy, and up to **16** feet!

Anything that can spray you with its butt up to six times from across the room is something worth avoiding at all costs.

THE COCKROACH!

1. The cockroach is so hardy that some species can survive without food for a month, can be submerged for forty-five minutes or more without drowning, can regenerate lost limbs, and can even walk away after being nuked in a microwave.

2. The green banana cockroach is a popular pet because of its bright green color and ability to fly, while the Florida woods cockroach is not because of its ability to emit a very persistent, very foul odor.

3. The Central American giant cockroach is the heaviest insect in the world: It routinely grows to lengths of 5 inches or more, and can weigh in at nearly 60 grams, or about as much as eleven U.S. quarters.

1. **Fact.** Cockroaches truly are incredible little creatures. Perhaps most shocking is their ability to sometimes survive a microwave oven at full blast. There are two main explanations for the phenomenon:

First, roaches have very little water in their physical makeup. Microwave radiation causes water molecules in our TV dinners to vibrate, which causes friction, and, consequently, heat.

Second, microwave ovens do not spread their heating power uniformly throughout the chamber. Many have carousels to keep the food moving through the most intense focus points of the heat. A savvy cockroach can actually flee to the coolest parts of the oven.

---

2. **Fact.** The green banana cockroach is lime green and generally not regarded as a pest since they prefer to remain outdoors. They are very strong flyers.

The Florida woods cockroach is often called a palmetto bug or a skunk roach.

3. **Bullsh*t!** The heaviest insect in the world is the **goliath beetle**, native to Africa, which can grow to more than 4 inches long and weigh in at 100 grams or more, which is about the **weight of a newborn kitten**.

The heaviest cockroach is the Australian burrowing cockroach, which can reach 3.5 inches in length, and weigh in at 30 grams. The Central American giant cockroach routinely grows to the same length, but is nowhere near as heavy.

Fact. Fact. **Bullsh*t!**

THE BABOON!

1. Baboons are large terrestrial monkeys with a dog-like muzzle. Unlike many monkeys, they do not have a prehensile tail. There are five species of baboon, and they are some of the largest examples of non-hominid primates.

2. The reason that many baboons have bright red butts is because of their accretion disc, a large, sensitive gland that regulates hormones in the primate's body. It serves a dual purpose — a baboon flashing its crimson rear end is a signal of aggression and a warning to potential predators.

3. In Egyptian mythology, Babi was a baboon god. Babi was bloodthirsty and a consumer of souls, and one of the gods of the underworld. Babi was also believed to be the god of the virility *of the dead*. Ancient Egyptians would pray to Babi in order to avoid impotence in the afterlife.

1. **Fact.** Baboons are Old World monkeys. New World monkeys are known for their prehensile tails, which are tails that have adapted to gripping, grasping, and manipulating objects. Baboons have tails, but cannot grip anything with them.

    The five species of baboon are the chacma baboon, the guinea baboon, the olive baboon, the yellow baboon, and the hamadryas baboon.

2. **Bullsh*t!** When a baboon displays its backside, it is a sign of **submission**, not aggression. When females are ready to mate, their bums will get pinker and more swollen, and she will display it. Males will even present their butts to other males when they want to capitulate.

    Baboon rear ends are protruding because of **ischial callosities**, which is a fancy name for calluses. They make the baboon's bum less sensitive, so they can sit for long periods of time and even sleep while sitting in a tree.

    Accretion discs are structures formed by diffuse material in orbit around a central body, such as a star or black hole. They are space phenomena and have absolutely nothing to do with baboon butts.

3. **Fact.** *Babi* or *Baba*, roughly translated, means "Bull of the Baboons." Babi was the son of Osiris, god of the dead, and was said to stand next to a lake of fire in the underworld and devour the souls of the unrighteous.

    Many ancient Egyptians believed that living baboons were actually dead ancestors.

THE HUMMINGBIRD!

1. The world's smallest living bird is the bee hummingbird, native to Cuba. The bee hummingbird grows to the same length as the short side of a standard business card and weighs less than one.

---

2. Hummingbirds have the highest metabolism of any living animal. The fastest heart rate ever measured in a hummingbird is 450 beats per minute. Fast living means fast dying: Hummingbirds have a lifespan of about a year.

---

3. Hummingbirds hover by beating their wings at an extremely high velocity—often as fast as 100 beats per second. Hummingbirds routinely fly at 30 miles per hour, and can dive at 60 miles per hour. They are the only species of bird that can fly backward.

1. Fact. The bee hummingbird grows to slightly less than 2 inches, and weighs less than 2 grams. That's less than the weight of a dime, and less than the combined weight of two one-dollar bills! (It's less than two hundred-dollar bills as well, for that matter.)

A bee hummingbird nest is about 1 inch wide, and bee hummingbird eggs are about the size of a pea.

2. Bullsh*t! You could only claim that hummingbirds have the highest metabolism of any animal if you exclude insects. A blue-throated hummingbird was once measured to have a heart rate of **1,260** beats per minute.

Such a high metabolism means hummingbirds have to consume several times their weight in nectar per day, and are constantly only hours away from death by starvation.

Still, they soldier on, and are longevity wonders when you take into account their incredible metabolic rate. Average American hummingbirds live for three to five years, and several species routinely live for longer than a decade. One hummingbird in captivity lived for **seventeen** years.

3. Fact. There is actually quite a range in wing beats per second—the giant hummingbird's wings beat about nine times per second, medium-sized species beat around twenty times per second, and the smallest species can get up to a hundred.

Hummingbirds can rotate their wings and actually get power from both the upstroke and the downstroke. As a consequence, they can hover and fly side to side, as well as forward and backward. No other birds can do this; physicists are actively studying hummingbirds in hopes of improving our own understanding of aerodynamics.

Fact. Fact. **Bullsh*t!**

THE PANDA!

1. Pandas are by far the most expensive animal to keep in American zoos. They are five times more costly than the elephant, which is the second most expensive.

---

2. Pandas, like all bears, are members of the scientific family Muridae. Their closest evolutionary relatives are dogs, of the family Canidae. The panda's closest living relative is *Ailurus fulgens*, or the red panda, which is extremely dog-like.

---

3. Pandas are notoriously reluctant to mate in captivity. Many outside-the-box methods to encourage reproduction have been attempted, including showing the lazy bears "panda porn" and even dosing them with Viagra.

1. **Fact.** The biggest culprit is the Chinese government, which regularly charges foreign zoos $1 million per year per panda on loan. If cubs are born, then China increases the price, by another $500,000 or so.

   Pandas require upwards of eighty pounds of bamboo per day for their diet, which only adds to the price tag.

2. **Bullsh*t!** Pandas, like all bears, are members of the scientific family **Ursidae**. (Muridae are mice.) Ursidae's closest relatives are the superfamily Pinnipedia, which, believe it or not, are comprised of **seals, walruses,** and **sea lions**.

   The panda's closest living relative is the South American spectacled bear.

   Dogs, walruses, bears, and skunks are all members of the suborder Caniformia, which means that bears and dogs are more closely related to each other than they are to other mammals such as rodents, cats, kangaroos, and humans.

   Red pandas are not bears at all, and they are extremely cat-like.

3. **Fact.** Panda breeders in China have all but torn their hair out in search of ways to encourage copulation. Among the many things they have tried are artificial insemination, special herbs, Viagra, and showing videos of pandas mating, popularly referred to as "panda porn."

THE COW!

1. The sport of cow-tipping has been debunked as being largely myth. It would be impossible for one or two people to tip over a full-sized, healthy cow. Five people could conceivably do it, but only if the cow were rigid and completely unresponsive, which is unlikely, since cows do not sleep standing up.

2. Cows have four stomachs, each of which perform a unique digestive function. They are called the triclinium, the caldarium, the apodyterium, and the puteus. The triclinium is the largest.

3. Cattle use 30 percent of the world's land surface (there is one cow for every five people on the planet), and are one of the very biggest contributors to harmful greenhouse gases in our atmosphere, even ahead of cars! The majority of the gas released comes from cow burps, farts, and poop.

1. **Fact.** Cows do not sleep standing up, but they can doze while chewing their cud. Still, cows are wary and easily disturbed, so sneaking up on one would be particularly difficult.

   According to a 2005 study by zoologists, tipping over a cow would require 2,910 newtons of force, or the equivalent of 4.43 people. This would require the cow to be as still as a statue. Cows, like most animals on legs, would brace themselves against the force, which would make them even more difficult to tip.

2. **Bullsh*t!** Technically, cows have **one** stomach with four compartments. They are called the rumen, the reticulum, the omasum, and the abomasum. The rumen is the largest.

   Triclinium, caldarium, apodyterium, and puteus are all **architectural features of ancient Roman bathhouses**.

3. **Fact.** There are an estimated 1.3 billion cattle in the world, and roughly 6.77 billion people.

   The automotive industry produces rawer CO_2 than livestock, but if you measure CO_2-equivalent gases, cattle production as a whole produces 18 percent of human-related greenhouse gases released into our atmosphere, which is more than cars. The livestock sector produces 37 percent of anthropogenic methane (which has twenty-three times the global warming potential of CO_2), 65 percent of anthropogenic nitrous oxide (296 times the global warming potential of CO_2), and 64 percent of anthropogenic ammonia emissions (which causes acid rain).

   The methane comes from "enteric fermentation," which is science speak for burps and farts, and the nitrous oxide comes from manure, a.k.a. poop.

THE SQUIRREL!

1. The Himalayan mole, the Florida water rat, and the pygmy beaver are not moles, rats, or beavers at all: They are actually each a species of squirrel.

2. A flying squirrel doesn't in fact fly, but glides from tree to tree. It does so with help from its patagium, a furry membrane that stretches between its limbs to form a kind of wing. It can use its tail as an airfoil, increasing drag when it needs to brake and land on a tree branch.

3. While most squirrels are known for eating seeds and nuts, the thirteen-lined ground squirrel, native to North America, is much more vicious: In addition to seeds and nuts, it is known to eat insects, birds, mice, snakes, and even other thirteen-lined ground squirrels.

1. **Bullsh*t!** The Himalayan mole is a mole, the Florida water rat is a muskrat, and the pygmy beaver does not exist.

But, believe it or not, the chipmunk, the marmot, and the prairie dog are all squirrels.

2. **Fact.** Flying squirrels have been recorded gliding as far as 295 feet!

Another good name for a flying squirrel is "bird food," since they are heavily preyed upon by nocturnal owls.

3. **Fact.** Thirteen-lined ground squirrels are omnivorous, and around 50 percent of their diet is meat.

As the name suggests, these squirrels have thirteen alternating brown and white lines running the length of their bodies. They are also sometimes known as the leopard squirrel, the striped gopher, or the squinney.

THE EARTHWORM!

1. Earthworms are hermaphrodites, and have both testes and ovaries. However, an earthworm cannot fertilize itself.

2. A study by Rothamsted Research suggests that rich farmland can have as many as 1,750,000 earthworms per acre, which means, on a dairy farm, the worms below can easily outweigh the livestock above.

3. The giant Palouse earthworm from Washington State is the world's longest species of earthworm, regularly growing to lengths of up to 7 feet.

1. **Fact.** Earthworms do copulate with each other to reproduce. When they do, both individuals release sperm to fertilize the other's eggs. Earthworms have a thick band, called a clitellum, which oozes a thick fluid sometime after copulation to make a cocoon. The earthworm deposits its own eggs and the other worm's sperm into the cocoon.

Some types of earthworm can reproduce by themselves via parthenogenesis. But this process is asexual and produces a clone.

---

2. **Fact.** Darwin, in his time, was a great student of the earthworm. He suggested that each acre of garden land contained 53,000 worms, a figure that Rothamsted Research has significantly increased with their recent findings.

According to Rothamsted, even poor soil can have as many as 250,000 worms per acre.

3. **Bullsh*t!** The world's longest earthworms are **African giant earthworms**, which have been recorded to grow as long as **22 feet** and can weigh in at more than 3 pounds.

The giant Palouse earthworm is still a shocking specimen—they are albino, sometimes more than an inch thick, and can grow up to 3½ feet long.

THE SNOW LEOPARD!

1. Classified as "small" cats, snow leopards make up for their diminutive size with a powerful jump: A snow leopard can leap 20 feet in a single bound.

2. Snow leopard tails are thicker and longer in proportion to their body than other big cats. These chunky tails are very useful in helping the snow leopard balance on steep slopes, and are wrapped around the body and face of the cat at night, acting effectively as a blanket.

3. The snow leopard is the symbol of the Girl Scouts Association of Kyrgyzstan.

1. **Bullsh*t!** Snow leopards are sometimes classified as **medium cats, and sometimes as large**. They can leap as far as **45** feet in a single bound (3 feet shy of the length between half court and a basketball net). This incredible bound is useful for the ambush, which is the preferred method of hunting for the snow leopard.

   Snow leopards are typically between 31 and 50 inches long, making them, mathematically, medium-sized. Other mediums are cougars, ocelots, lynxes, and mountain lions. Big cats such as lions and tigers are much larger than the snow leopard, and small cats, such as the Andean mountain cat and the margay, are much smaller.

   Like small cats, snow leopards purr but cannot roar.

2. **Fact.** Snow leopard tails are extremely flexible and can grow to more than a meter long, nearly as long as the cat itself! They are stocky with stores of fat. The mass of the tail makes it even more effective for balancing, and for face-warming at night.

3. **Fact.** Snow leopards carry a lot of symbolic meaning in Central Asia, where you'll find them on many coats of arms, badges, emblems, and even some currency.

THE ELEPHANT!

1. Elephants are the only surviving members of the scientific order Proboscidea, which once included the 26-foot-long *Stegodon*, the *Platybelodon* with its huge shovel-shaped tusks, the *Cuvieronius* with its long spiral-shaped tusks, the *Anancus* with tusks as long as its body, the huge and shaggy wooly mammoth, and the similarly hairy American mastodon.

2. We often see elephants as gentle giants, but in truth, they are often very aggressive, violent, and dangerous. Recently, in India, elephants have mounted raids against human villages, killing hundreds of people.

3. While the human body contains approximately 2,000 major muscles, there are nearly 10,000 muscles in an elephant's trunk alone!

1. **Fact.** Asian and African elephants are the only members left of what was a big, diverse family of enormous mammals.

   In English, we often facetiously use the term "proboscis" to mean nose, but it actually means "an elongated appendage on the head of an animal." A butterfly has a proboscis, as does an elephant, and you could make a case that my Uncle Mort does as well.

---

2. **Fact.** Elephants have been killing people and destroying villages in India, and, scarily, the incidents appear to be increasing in frequency. Many experts believe that the attacks are actually vindictive—a response to poaching and destruction of their habitat.

   Elephant violence and aggression aren't new, though. Trained war elephants were used in battle by the Greek general Pyrrhus of Epirus, and the Carthaginian military commander Hannibal.

3. **Bullsh*t!** In terms of major muscles, an elephant's trunk has **40,000**, and broken up into the individual muscle units, it has more than **100,000**!

   The human body only has between **600** and **900** major muscles, depending on your criteria.

   A full-sized elephant, with its trunk alone, can lift objects in the neighborhood of 500 pounds. The trunk is also dexterous and sensitive enough to pick a single blade of grass or take a coin from the ground.

THE MANATEE!

1. Manatees belong to the order Sirenia, which comes from the Latin *syreni*, meaning "mermaid." The name "manatee" is believed to be derived from the Carib word *manati*, which means "breast."

2. A manatee can grow as long as 12 feet and can weigh nearly 4,000 pounds! It makes sense that they can be so large—their closest living relative is the elephant.

3. While Florida manatees typically swim too deep to be threatened by recreational boat traffic, there have been a handful of cases where manatees have been injured by collisions with hulls and propellers. Recently, an individual manatee was discovered with scar patterns from a record three separate boat collisions.

1. **Fact.** It's a common theory that the mermaid sightings of Christopher Columbus's day were, in fact, sea cow sightings. Manatees do have mammary glands near their armpits.

---

2. **Fact.** Manatees are mammals, and are believed to have evolved from four-legged land creatures some 60 million years ago. They are closely related to the order Proboscidea (the elephants) as well as the order Hyracoidea (the hyraxes). Manatees have a prehensile upper lip that shows similar properties to an elephant trunk, though it's not nearly as long!

Though manatees can grow to be 12 feet long and weigh nearly 4,000 pounds, an average one would be a little over 9 feet long and weight around 1,000 pounds.

3. **Bullsh*t!** Manatees typically graze at a depth of 3 to 6 feet, and are frequently mutilated, maimed, and occasionally killed by collisions with boats and boat propellers.

It is common to discover manatees bearing the scar patterns of more than **ten** separate boat or propeller collisions, and one was discovered with evidence of more than **fifty** separate collisions.

Many individuals have been observed with gruesome disfigurements due to the slicing-and-dicing of motorboat propellers, including gaping wounds, severed tails, and exposed lungs.

The manatees are tough, however, and, amazingly, often survive.

THE TYRANNOSAURUS!

1. *Tyrannosaurus rex* was a coelurosaur of the Saurischian order, and of the suborder Theropod, from which all modern birds evolved. Cousins to the *Tyrannosaurus*, all modern birds (including my pet parakeet, Stanley) are dinosaurs.

2. The *Tyrannosaurus* was one of the largest land carnivores ever, and could grow to over 40 feet long and 13 feet tall at the hip. There were larger bipedal carnivores, however, including the *Spinosaurus* and the *Gigantosaurus*, both of which looked very similar to *T. rex*.

3. *T. rex* was dominant during the Jurassic period, which lasted from about 250 million to 200 million years ago and saw the dawn of dinosaurs.

1. **Fact.** Although there is still some token scientific dissent to the idea, most paleontologists now agree that birds are avian dinosaurs. The evidence is strong enough now that we feel confident calling it truth.

   T. rex was a member of Coelurosauria, which is a group ("clade") of theropod dinosaurs closely related to birds. *T. rex* was a saurischian, which means "lizard-hipped." All carnivorous dinosaurs were saurischians.

   Finally, *Tyrannosaurus* was a theropod, which describes both a suborder of carnivorous saurischian dinosaurs, and the clade of those dinosaurs and their descendents, including birds.

---

2. **Fact.** The *Gigantosaurus* was slightly larger than *Tyrannosaurus*, but its brain was half as big. *Spinosaurus* was bigger than both *Tyrannosaurus* and *Gigantosaurus*, and had a big, scary "sail" of elongated spinal bones.

3. **Bullsh*t!** Although the movie *Jurassic Park* implies otherwise, *Tyrannosaurus* did not live during the Jurassic period. It came much later, in the Cretaceous period.

   The Triassic period, not the Jurassic, was 200 to 350 million years ago, and the first dinosaurs appeared then. The Jurassic (or the Age of Reptiles) was about 200 to 145 million years ago, and the Cretaceous was about 145 to 65 million years ago. All three periods make up the Mesozoic era.

   T. rex existed during the tail end of the Cretaceous, in the vicinity of 67 million years ago, and was one of the last non-avian dinosaurs to walk the earth before the major extinction event.

THE SWAN!

1. The largest native North American bird (by weight and length) is the trumpeter swan, which can tip the scales at 38 pounds, can grow to be 6 feet long, and have a nearly 10-foot wingspan. It is the largest waterfowl on earth.

---

2. Swans may look pure, but they are actually quite promiscuous, mating often and with many partners. Most species of swan are polygamous: During a breeding season, a female will mate with several males, with the result that a single clutch of eggs could have several fathers.

---

3. In England, all unmarked mute swans are technically property of the Crown. There is an annual ceremonial swan census on the River Thames called "Swan Upping." A crew of Royal Swan Uppers in scarlet uniforms row for five days, all the while counting swans, and are led by a man with the prestigious title of "the Queen's Swan Marker."

1. **Fact.** Turkeys can be heavier, and the California condor can have a wider wingspan, but the trumpeter swan is larger than both when you count all factors.

   The largest bird in the world is the ostrich, which can grow to 9 feet tall and weigh 400 pounds. The largest bird ever was the elephant bird of Madagascar, now extinct, that could have weighed up to 900 pounds and was regularly more than 10 feet tall.

2. **Bullsh*t!** Swans have long been one of the shining examples of **monogamy** in the animal kingdom. A swan will form a bond with one partner that can last for many years, and sometimes for life. This is one of the main reasons that swans are a symbol of love.

   Our cherished view of the sanctity of swan "marriage" is under attack, however, as recent studies have shown swan "divorce" to be more common than previously thought, and mute swans have been documented to form same-sex bonds.

3. **Fact.** The tradition began in the twelfth century, when swans were a rare and royal delicacy for the dinner table. Today, the tradition is upheld for the sake of conservation.

   When the Royal Swan Uppers pass Windsor Castle, the rowers stand at attention in the boat and salute "Her Majesty the Queen, Seigneur of the Swans."

Fact. Fact. **Bullsh*t!**

THE OTTER!

1. Otters are in the same biological family as badgers, polecats, weasels, stoats, minks, and wolverines.

---

2. Giant otters, also known as river dogs, are native to the Gulf of San Jorge, off the coast of Argentina. A fully grown male giant otter is typically between 7 and 8 feet long, and will weigh upwards of 300 pounds!

---

3. Sea otters have the thickest fur of any animal in the world, boasting between 600,000 and 1 million hairs per square inch. Altogether, each sea otter has around 800 million hairs on its body.

1. **Fact.** Otters and the others are members of the family Mustelidae, from the Latin *mustela*, for "weasel."

   Although they all share the same family, biologists believe otters are most closely related to minks and weasels.

2. **Bullsh*t!** Don't be ridiculous. Giant otters, also known as water dogs, and in South America as river wolfs, aren't that giant. They're native to the Amazon River, in the northern half of South America. Males are about **5 feet long** and weigh about **80 pounds**.

   There are reports of giant otter skins measuring over 7 feet, but this size is not typical, and has not been seen in quite some time, likely a result of the big guys being poached.

   Sea otters often weigh more than giant otters, tipping the scales at up to 100 pounds.

3. **Fact.** If you're wondering just how hairy that really is, we typically have about 100,000 to 150,000 hairs on our **whole head**. (Unless you're bald as a doorknob, like me.)

   Sea otters' fur is so thick that their skin doesn't get wet when they swim. This makes up for the fact that they have no blubber to keep them warm as seals do.

   Sea otters are one of the only non-primate species of mammal in the world that uses tools. They use rocks to break open the shells of clams, mussels, snails, and crabs to get to the tasty morsels inside.

THE SHARK!

1. The smallest species of shark is the dwarf lanternshark, which is typically between 6 and 7 inches long. The largest is the whale shark, which can grow longer than 40 feet, and is also the largest existing species of fish.

---

2. Sharks have the hardest bones of any fish. Recovered shark ribs, naturally pointed, were believed to be among the first tools used by our prehuman ancestors.

---

3. One of the rarest species of fish in the sea is the megamouth shark, which was only discovered in 1976. In the decades since then, there have been fewer than 100 sightings or specimens reported. Scientists still know very little about the big, flabby bottom-feeder.

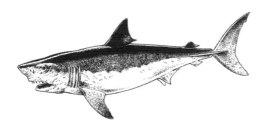

1. **Fact.** The longest known dwarf lanternshark was 8.3 inches. The little guys have only been spotted in a relatively small area of the Caribbean, off the coasts of Colombia and Venezuela.

   The longest known whale shark was measured at 41.5 feet. The heaviest recorded weighed in at more than 79,000 pounds!

2. **Bullsh*t!** Sharks, like rays and skates, are **cartilaginous fish**— a shark skeleton has no bone, and is made up of cartilage and connective tissue, roughly half the density of bone. Sharks are very unique in this way: The vast majority of fish are Osteichthyes, which do have bony skeletons.

   On top of that, sharks **have no rib cage** at all. Because of this, a shark on land would be in great danger of being crushed by its own body weight.

3. **Fact.** The megamouth is aptly named, since it is characterized by its large head and big rubbery lips. By 2010, only fifty sightings or specimens had been reported of the megamouth, making it a rare fish indeed.

   In 2009, Philippine fishermen accidentally caught one of these monsters of the deep in their nets. They promptly sautéed it in coconut milk and declared it delicious.

Fact. Fact. **Bullsh*t!**

THE KOALA!

1. Koalas are herbaceous omnivores, native to Western Australia and Tasmania. Dependent on the rainforest for survival, they are a critically endangered species.

2. The male koala has a bifurcated penis (two for the price of one!), and female koalas have two lateral vaginas and two uteri.

3. Koalas sleep between sixteen and twenty-two hours per day, because of their incredibly slow metabolism and their poor diet. They spend between two and five hours a day eating.

1. **Bullsh*t!** Koalas live in **woodlands**, not rainforests. They are native to eastern and southern Australia, and are not found in Western Australia or Tasmania. Koalas are not herbaceous (the word describes plants), and they are not omnivores, but **herbivores**.

    They are also not critically endangered, but there may be fewer than 100,000 individuals in the wild.

2. **Fact.** Strange but true. Most male marsupials have some version of this "double" penis. Female koalas have a "vaginal apparatus" that consists of two lateral vaginas, each connected to a separate uterus.

---

3. **Fact.** Koalas subsist entirely on leaves, their favorite being eucalyptus leaves. It is an odd choice, since eucalyptus leaves are low in protein and high in toxins and indigestible fibrous matter. Having a low metabolism and sleeping quite a bit help koalas conserve the massive amount of energy they need to digest and process such difficult food.

THE LIGER!

1. Hybrid cats such as the liger, a cross between a male tiger and a lioness, are completely infertile. In the wild, a liger could never happen: It takes human intervention, veterinary attention, and careful planning in captivity to create the delicate conditions appropriate for a lion and tiger to successfully mate.

2. Ligers are the largest cats in the world. Hercules, a 900-plus pound, 12-foot-long liger from South Carolina, holds the Guinness World Record for biggest living cat and is larger than both his parents *combined*.

3. Ligers are far from alone in the hybrid big-cat animal kingdom. There have been confirmed cases of jaglions, liguars, leoliguars, jagupards, leguars, lijaguleps, leopons, lipards, leoligulors, and tigards.

1. **Bullsh*t!** Ligers and their counterparts, tiglons, were long thought to be infertile, but this turns out to be **incorrect**. Male ligers and tiglons are sterile, but females are often fertile. In one example, a 1975 pairing between a lion and a female liger resulted in a cub (referred to as a li-liger) that was successfully raised to adulthood.

   The liger, by the way, is a hybrid cross between a **male lion and a tigress**. When a male tiger and a lioness mate, the result is a **tiglon**. Ligers are much more common in zoos and parks today than tiglons.

   It does not take human intervention or careful planning for ligers to be produced. In fact, **most of the ligers in captivity were produced by accident**. In the wild, lion and tiger mating is extremely unlikely, mainly because lion and tiger habitats, in general, don't overlap. But it *could* happen, and many biologists think it has.

2. **Fact.** Ligers' huge size is a result of hybrid vigor, which means Hercules inherited the best traits from both species. Hercules is said to be able to run at 50 miles per hour and to eat more than 25 pounds of meat a day.

---

3. **Fact.** All are very real. My favorites are the lijagulep, the result of a male lion mating with a female jagupard or leguar, and the leoligulor, the result of a male leopon (which is actually fertile) mating with a liguar.

   Zebroids (zebra and horse), pizzlies (polar bear and grizzly bear), and wholpins (dolphin and false killer whale) are all real too.

THE UNICORN!

1. While the mythical unicorn never existed, the single-horned monoceros did. Last observed by Dutch biologist Petrus Plancius in 1613, sightings of the monoceros, a nomadic antilocaprid most closely related to the giraffe, were extremely rare, and usually at night.

---

2. In 1663, in Germany's Harz Mountains, a fossilized skeleton was constructed that appeared to be a unicorn. It was assembled by scientist and inventor Otto von Guericke, and later examined by philosopher and mathematician Gottfried Leibniz, both of whom concluded that it was, in fact, a unicorn.

---

3. A "unicorn bull," with a large single horn growing out of the middle of its head, was the wonder of a 1933 cow herd. The "unicorn" was the undisputed leader of all the other bulls, and it had the same gentle, docile temperament that is often attributed to the mythical unicorn.

1. **Bullsh*t!** Monoceros, first observed by Dutch **cartographer** Petrus Plancius in 1612 or 1613, is a **constellation on the celestial equator**. *Monoceros* is Greek for "unicorn."

    Antilocaprids were real horned mammals related to giraffes, and the only existing one today is the North American pronghorn. The pronghorn has two horns.

2. **Fact.** The skeleton had no hindquarters and was missing part of its spine. Still, spectators flocked to the ridiculous-looking thing.

    Modern analysis revealed the skeleton to be a combination of mammoth and rhinoceros bones.

---

3. **Fact.** The "unicorn bull" existed, but was not a product of nature. Dr. W. Franklin Dove of Maine University actually used surgery to produce the unicorn effect. When the bull was a calf, Dove removed the two horn buds and replaced them in the center of the skull. As the horns grew, they fused together, making a single large, straight horn.

    The spear on the bull's head was a very effective weapon, and the other bulls quickly learned not to challenge the unicorn. As a result of being secure in his power, the bull developed a very gentle manner.

Fact. Fact. **Bullsh*t!**

CHAPTER 2

Pop Culture!

I know a bestselling, prize-winning author who is hopelessly addicted to reality TV shows about rich housewives, and a decorated sommelier who has Bieber fever. These days, Americans watch three to eight hours of television every day—much more time than we spend socializing. At the supermarket, you can find a mountain of magazines with cover stories about what color toothbrush your favorite celebrity uses.

Of course, popular culture is more than just tacky television and celebrities—it's the music we listen to, the lingo we use, the clothes we wear, the cars we drive. If you think you're not connected to pop culture, take a look at photographs of people a hundred years ago and ask yourself: Do I look like them? A hundred years from now, somebody may look at a picture of *you* and say, "What is she *wearing*? What is that strange machine next to her? And what does that gesture mean?"

If you've been a college student recently, you might well have taken a "Philosophy and Star Trek" course at Georgetown University, or perhaps Brooklyn College's "*South Park* and Political Correctness." You might have enjoyed Frostburg State University's "The Science of *Harry Potter*," Stanford's "Psychology of Facebook," or if you're truly masochistic, the University of Virginia's "GaGa for Gaga: Sex, Gender, and Identity."

And if you've taken them *all*, you might be ready to spot the bullshit in this chapter.

BACK TO THE FUTURE!

1. In Robert Zemeckis and Bob Gale's original draft of the script, the time machine was a modified Honda CBX 650 motorcycle. In order to generate the power needed to return home, Marty and Doc had to steal atomic energy from a nearby nuclear reactor.

---

2. Michael J. Fox was originally considered to be too busy shooting *Family Ties* to be in the film, so the producers cast Eric Stoltz instead. Stoltz filmed the role for a month before he was fired and Fox was cast.

---

3. President Ronald Reagan was a huge fan of the movie. During a personal screening, he laughed uproariously at Doc Brown's joke at his expense and had the projectionist run the scene again. Reagan went on to quote the movie in his 1986 State of the Union address.

1. **Bullsh*t!** In the original draft of the script, the time machine was a **refrigerator**. In order to return home, Marty and Doc had to harness power from an atomic explosion at the Nevada Test Site. Zemeckis scrapped the idea because he was concerned kids would lock themselves in refrigerators after seeing the movie.

2. **Fact.** Recasting the part added $3 million to the price tag of the film. Fox continued shooting *Family Ties* during the day and shot *Back to the Future* on nights and weekends. Stoltz, it was decided, was too dramatic as Marty McFly. Teen heartthrob Corey Hart was also considered for the part. The filmmakers' original choice for Doc Brown? John Lithgow.

3. **Fact.** The affable president quoted Doc Brown: "Where we're going, we don't need roads." Richard Nixon also had a connection to the movie: He attended Whittier High School, which served as the set for the film's fictional Hill Valley High School.

Fact. Fact. **Bullsh*t!**

THE CELL PHONE!

1. The first cell phone call was placed in New York City in 1973 by Dr. Martin Cooper on a Motorola phone that weighed more than 4 pounds. The first mobile phone call was placed in St. Louis in 1946 with a phone plus equipment that weighed 80 pounds.

2. In 1987, around 1 million people in the U.S. had a cell phone. By 2010, more than 285 million people in the country had one. That means Americans with cell phones today outnumber the total population of the country in 1987 by many millions.

3. A recent study revealed that around one in 200 British people suffer from nomophobia: the persistent, irrational fear of cell phones. Nomophobes will go to great lengths to avoid owning or even using cell phones, and they experience anxiety while near one, even if the phone is off.

1. **Fact.** Dr. Cooper developed the phone for Motorola, and had the honor of placing the first call. The battery alone weighed as much as five entire cell phones today, and only lasted twenty minutes.

   In 1946, a *cell* phone hadn't been conceived of, but a *mobile* phone had. The phone operated using the Mobile Telephone Service, which was actually radio-based. In 1946, there were only three channels available for mobile phone calls, which meant that each one was a sort of party line. The service cost $30 per month, which, adjusted for inflation, is the equivalent of more than $300 today.

   Then, of course, there would be the chiropractor fees you'd need to pay after lugging around 80 pounds of equipment.

---

2. **Fact.** There are well over 307 million American citizens around today, over 90 percent of whom have a cell phone. In 1987, the population of the country was between 230 and 245 million people total.

   In 2009, Americans used about 6.1 billion minutes of talk time each day.

3. **Bullsh*t!** Nomophobia is quite real, but it is the fear of **being out of cell phone contact**. Nomophobes experience anxiety when **away from their phones**, often **never turn them off**, and experience noticeable increases in anxiety and stress levels **when their battery is low**. "Nomophobia" is a portmanteau of "no-mobile-phobia." A recent study found that **53 percent** of Brits are nomophobes.

RUBIK'S CUBE!

1. A classic Rubik's Cube has 43,252,003,274,489,856,000 possible starting positions. If you had a Rubik's Cube for every possible permutation, you could cover the surface of 30,000 earths.

2. The Rubik's Cube was first invented by naval engineer Richard James in the 1940s, who first called it "The Rubric Cube." His two sons couldn't pronounce it, calling it "Rubik's Cube" instead, and the new name stuck.

3. A Saturday-morning cartoon called *Rubik, the Amazing Cube* ran for one season in 1983. The show centered on three siblings, Carlos, Lisa, and Reynaldo Rodriguez, and their magical talking cube named Rubik. The theme song was recorded by the boy band Menudo.

1. **Fact.** When the toys first went on sale, promotional materials stated that there were "more than 3 billion" possible arrangements of a Rubik's Cube. This was correct, since there are more than 43 quintillion arrangements, but it's a gross understatement—it's even more extreme than saying the earth is home to more than one person.

   If you counted the permutations of the Rubik's Cube at a rate of one per second, it would take you even longer than the total age of the universe. Much longer.

   Despite the ridiculously high number of combinations, a team of mathematicians proved in 2010 that you are never more than twenty moves away from solving a Rubik's Cube.

2. **Bullsh*t!** Richard James, a naval engineer, did invent one of the most popular toys of all time in the 1940s: **the Slinky**.

   The Rubik's Cube was **invented in 1974** by a **Hungarian architect named Ernő Rubik**.

3. **Fact.** Rubik looked a lot like a Smurf trapped in a regular Rubik's Cube toy. He had all kinds of magical powers, and routinely saved Carlos, Lisa, and Reynaldo from an evil magician. Before Rubik could unleash his magical powers, he had to be solved.

   Episodes include "Honolulu Rubik," "Back Packin' Rubik," and "Rubik and the Pooch-Nappers."

THE BEATLES!

1. Before joining the Beatles, Ringo Starr played in a very short-lived band called Beatcomber, alongside Roy Dyke, Richie Snare, Billy Shears, and Richard Starkey.

2. There was a fifth Beatle, named Stuart Sutcliffe, who tragically died of an aneurysm at age twenty-one in 1962. In the same year, the Beatles's original drummer, Pete Best, was replaced by Ringo Starr.

3. The original name for the song "Hey Jude" was "Hey Julos," and was about Julian Lennon, John's son. In 1996, Julian anonymously bid £25,000 at an auction to get the original recording notes for the song.

2. **Fact.** Sutcliffe was the band's bassist who quit in 1961 to pursue his visual art career. Some believe that his aneurysm in 1962 was a result of an earlier bar fight he had gotten into alongside John Lennon in 1961. The true cause is not known.

   Pete Best was the drummer for the Beatles from August 1960 to August 1962.

3. **Fact.** Paul McCartney wrote the song for Julian shortly after John split up with Julian's mother, Cynthia, in hopes that it would help him cope. McCartney later changed the name in the song to "Jude" because it "sounded better."

   Julian Lennon was famously bitter towards his father for years, but in the '90s he started to acquire mementos (such as the "Hey Jude" recording notes) and publicly started to embrace his connection to John.

SOAP OPERAS!

1. The term "soap opera" originated in the 1950s, during the dawn of daytime serials, as a disparaging reference to the idea that the audience was made up of procrastinating laundrywomen and dish-washing housewives.

2. The longest-running television drama of all time was *Guiding Light*, which was canceled in 2009 after fifty-seven years and nearly 16,000 episodes. Second place goes to *As the World Turns*, with fifty-four years and nearly 14,000 episodes.

3. Soap operas are not just an American phenomenon. They are hugely popular in the United Kingdom and Australia, and, in all, soap operas are aired in more than fifty countries, including Kazakhstan, Jamaica, Indonesia, Egypt, and Slovakia.

1. **Bullsh*t!** The term originated in the **1930s**, and it was disparaging, but in actuality the word "soap" was a reference to the fact that the shows were sponsored by manufacturers of **household cleaning products**, such as Procter & Gamble. "Opera" was a reference to the over-dramatic quality of the programs. The first soap operas were **radio broadcasts**.

    Soap operas made the leap from the airwaves to the TV set during the 1950s, and by the early 1960s, radio soaps were all but extinct.

2. **Fact.** In fact, *Guiding Light* has the record for the longest-running drama in television and radio history. The show was launched on the radio in 1937, long before it made the jump to television in 1952. The show ran, in various formats, for seventy-two years. Between 1952 and 1956, *Guiding Light* was produced on both radio and television simultaneously.

    Both *As the World Turns* and *Guiding Light* were sponsored throughout their history by Procter & Gamble, the "soap" in "soap opera."

3. **Fact.** Sri Lanka, Belgium, Morocco, Japan, Estonia, China, New Zealand, and Serbia have their own soaps as well, as do many, many other countries.

    In 2011, the British soap *Coronation Street* was the longest-running soap opera still in production, having launched in 1960.

BARBIE!

1. Ruth Handler had the idea for Barbie dolls while on a 1956 trip to Germany, when she encountered a doll called Bild Lilli, which was for adults. She named Barbie after her daughter and Ken after her son.

---

2. Karate Barbie, Rodeo Clown Barbie, Grunge Barbie, and Twinkie-Time Barbie are all real, official Barbies produced by Mattel at one time or other.

---

3. The BBC News estimated that if Barbie were a real woman with the same proportions, and had a 28" waist, she would be 7'6" tall. A group of researchers at the University Central Hospital in Helsinki, Finland, similarly concluded that if Barbie were a real woman, she'd lack the 17 to 22 percent body fat required for regular menstruation.

1. **Fact.** Bild Lilli was based on a German cartoon character—a single sassy girl who was into the party scene and used men for money. The Bild Lilli doll was sold to adults as a joke gift. The original Barbie doll is extremely similar, with only a few modifications.

   Ruth Handler's husband had founded Mattel, and she would later become president of the company. She noticed her daughter giving her baby dolls adult roles during playtime, and decided girls needed adult dolls. She bought a few Bild Lilli dolls in Germany, brought them home, and the rest is toy history.

   Her children were named Barbara and Ken.

2. **Bullsh*t!** None of the mentioned were ever official Mattel Barbies, but Totally Tattoos Barbie, Oreo Fun Barbie, *The Birds* Barbie (styled after the Alfred Hitchcock movie, complete with attacking birds), Harley Davidson Barbie, NASCAR Barbie, Barbie's pregnant friend Midge, and the Barbie & Tanner play set (which includes her dog, a trash can, a scooper, and a tiny piece of dog poop) are all very, very real.

3. **Fact.** Barbie defenders argue that her proportions have to be exaggerated in order to wear doll clothes, which are much thicker in proportion to the body than human-sized clothes. Barbie's T-shirt, scaled to human size, would be as thick as a heavy coat.

   The 7'6" Barbie of BBC News's estimation would also have 40" hips and a 37" bust. Barbie creator Ruth Handler reportedly argued that it was important for a girl's esteem to play with a doll with breasts.

JEANS!

1. In 1909, Solomon Levi and William Strauss patented an amazing new kind of fabric—denim—and began selling blue jeans under the company name Levi Strauss. Andrew Strauss, the great-grandson of William, is the current C.E.O.

2. For a long time in the U.S., jeans were more popularly called dungarees, a name derived from Dungri, India, where a denim-like material was made. In Danish they are called *cowbuybusker*, and in Hungarian, *farmernadrág*.

3. After President Barack Obama threw the first pitch at the 2009 All Star game in a pair of ill-fitting Levi's, he was derided by the press for wearing "dad jeans." Obama responded to the outcry, saying, "Those jeans are comfortable. And for those of you who want your president to look great in his tight jeans, I'm sorry. I'm not the guy."

1. **Bullsh*t!** The company was founded (as a dry goods purveyor) **in 1853** by **Levi Strauss**, a Bavarian immigrant to the United States. He did not invent denim—it had been around for hundreds of years already. John Anderson is the C.E.O. of Levi Strauss & Co., not Andrew Strauss, who is a British cricket player.

   You generally can't patent a fabric, and it's even hard to obtain a patent on a style of clothing. Levi Strauss and his partner Jacob Davis did get a patent in 1873 for an "Improvement in Fastening Pocket-Openings," which was the method of using little copper rivets to reinforce work pants—a feature we still have on our jeans today.

   It is generally accepted that Levi Strauss & Co. was the first American company making and selling blue jeans.

2. **Fact.** Dungri (sometimes *Dongri*) is part of Mumbai, in India, and coarse calico (similar to denim but not the same) was made there for a long time, as were pants of the material.

   Apparently, Danes associate jeans with cowboys, while Hungarians associate them with farmers.

---

3. **Fact.** Obama went on to say, "Michelle—she looks fabulous. I'm a little frumpy." Critics complained that the pants were too baggy and high-waisted, and that the legs were too short.

   Obama threw the first pitch at Nationals Park on April 5, 2010, wearing sharp-looking, well-tailored khaki pants.

STAR WARS!

1. The original Star Wars trilogy earned a combined six Academy Awards and ten nominations, while the subsequent trilogy received three nominations and not a single Oscar. Still, the Star Wars franchise is the highest-grossing film series of all time.

---

2. When Darth Vader's iconic mask was first designed, it was only supposed to appear in one small scene in the initial film.

---

3. In Britain's 2001 census, 390,000 people listed "Jedi" as their religious affiliation. Inspired by this, the Church of Jediism was founded in 2008 as a legitimate religion for practitioners of "the Force." A British man narrowly avoided jail after donning a trash bag, yelling "Darth Vader!", and assaulting the leader of the church with a metal crutch.

1. **Bullsh*t!** The original Star Wars trilogy **did not win a single Oscar**, though it received six nominations. The later trilogy received **twenty nominations** for Academy Awards.

   Star Wars is the **third**-highest-grossing film series of all time, after Harry Potter and James Bond.

   Just in case you were wondering (I was), the Police Academy movies are rock-solid at around 135th place.

2. **Fact.** Originally, Vader was supposed to be a tall, grim-faced general. Since a scene involved him crossing through the vacuum of space to board a ship, a breathing apparatus was needed. Concept artist Ralph McQuarrie designed the helmet for the one scene. Little did he know that it would become an enduring cultural icon.

3. **Fact.** Although the 390,000 census respondents were making a collective joke, the Church of Jediism is very real. To date, they have over 16,000 official members of the church. The founder, Barnaby Jones, did take a mighty thwack to the head from a crutch. His attacker, Arwel Hughes, claimed to not remember the assault because he had drunk two gallons of boxed wine.

STAR TREK!

1. In the Star Trek franchise, aliens known as the Klingons periodically speak Klingon, which is a grammatically complete artificially constructed international auxiliary language created by linguist L. L. Zamenhof. Notable writers Baldur Ragnarsson, Marjorie Boulton, and Raymond Schwartz have all penned poetry in Klingon, and the horror movie *Incubus* was produced entirely in Klingon.

2. After playing Lieutenant Uhura on the first season of the original Star Trek series, Nichelle Nichols was seriously considering quitting the show. She was convinced to stay by Dr. Martin Luther King, Jr., who told her she was an invaluable role model for black women in America.

3. You could live on Star Trek Drive in either Birmingham, Alabama, or Shingletown, California; Star Trek Lane in Garland, Texas; Klingon Court in Sacramento, California; or Roddenberry Avenue (Star Trek was created by Gene Roddenberry) in Enterprise, Nevada.

1. **Bullsh*t!** Most of those statements are true about a different language, **Esperanto**. Klingon is not an international auxiliary language because it was not designed to facilitate communication between people who have different native languages. Esperanto was designed for this purpose, as were the Universalglot, Solresol, and Volapük languages.

   Klingon is popular in its own right, however: A 2010 production of Charles Dickens's *A Christmas Carol* was performed entirely in Klingon, the heavy metal band Stovokor performs entirely in Klingon, and the opera *'u'* was written and performed entirely in Klingon.

   You can even Google in Klingon.

2. **Fact.** The fact that Nichols, an African American, played a major role in a 1966 television show was not insignificant. Nichols recalled her encounter with King: "He said, 'You have the first non-stereotypical role in television. It's not a maid's role, it's not a menial role. . . . This is something that is the reason we are walking, we are marching.'"

   Uhura's kiss with Captain Kirk in a 1968 episode is popularly regarded as the first scripted interracial television kiss. Nichols would go on to be recruited by NASA to help encourage African-American women to become astronauts.

3. **Fact.** You can find them all on Google Maps. Clearly, some urban planners are fans.

TETRIS!

1. Tetris was first invented in 1984 by Alexey Pajitnov, a computer programmer at the Academy of Science of the USSR in Moscow. An early release of the game was called "TETЯIS: The Soviet Mind Game."

2. Tetris is the most popular video game of all time, having sold as many as 150 million units in its various forms.

3. A 2009 study by the Mind Research Network, hoping to prove that playing Tetris was beneficial, actually discovered that playing the game repetitively is harmful to the brain's development process.

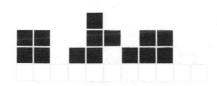

1. **Fact.** Perhaps there is a secret Communist message in Tetris.

2. **Fact.** You could argue the point of Tetris being the most "popular" game, but the numbers certainly don't lie. From 2005 to 2011 alone, more than 100 million Tetris downloads were sold just for mobile phones. For reference, the original Super Mario Bros. for the Nintendo Entertainment System was one of the most popular games ever, and sold around 40 million copies. Tetris debuted a year before Super Mario Bros.

    Tetris is the only game to be released on nearly every video game platform in existence, and can even be played on some non-video-game systems, including calculators, Internet radio devices, and *oscilloscopes*.

3. **Bullsh*t!** Not only did the Mind Research Network for Neuro-diagnostic Discovery study prove that playing Tetris on a regular basis **improved brain function**, the nonprofit was alarmed to discover that playing Tetris regularly can **make your brain bigger**.

    The study, conducted entirely on adolescent girls, showed markedly improved brain efficiency in the regions of the brain associated with critical thinking, reasoning, and language after three months of regularly playing Tetris. The girls also developed noticeably thicker cortexes in two regions of the brain—the parts associated with multisensory integration and planning complex movements.

    As a result of the evidence, some researchers believe that playing Tetris could also help aging and elderly brains, by slowing down deterioration.

    A half hour of Tetris a day keeps dementia away!

ZOMBIES!

1. Our modern conception of zombies as shambling, flesh-eating creatures is almost entirely due to George Romero's seminal 1968 movie *Night of the Living Dead*. However, the word "zombie" never appears in the film.

2. *Zombies Ate My Neighbors*, *Dead Head Fred*, *Zombie Panic in Wonderland*, *Voodoo Kid*, and *Little Red Riding Hood's Zombie BBQ* are all zombie movies that came out in 1987.

3. An *actual* "zombie" named Clairvius Narcisse wandered, glassy-eyed, back into his native Haitian village in 1980, even though he had been pronounced dead in 1962. He was recognized by many relatives and acquaintances who had attended his funeral and witnessed his burial.

1. **Fact.** Before *Night of the Living Dead*, zombies were typically portrayed in popular media as living people enslaved by witch doctors. Romero's vision of the malevolent walking dead lay the foundation for most renditions of zombies we see today.

   The word "zombie" is not in the film at all. The creatures are referred to as ghouls.

2. **Bullsh*t!** All of those are **zombie video games**.

   The year 1987 was still good for zombie movies, however: *I Was a Teenage Zombie, Zombie Vs. Ninja, Night of the Living Babes, Zombie High, Revenge of the Living Dead Girls*, and *The Video Dead* are all examples of zombie films that came out that year.

3. **Fact.** The very word "zombie" is borrowed from West Africa or Haiti or both, and can mean either the walking dead or a person in an entranced state.

   The story of the Haitian zombie Clairvius Narcisse was heavily investigated by Harvard-trained anthropologist and ethnobotanist Wade Davis in the '80s, resulting in his book *The Serpent and the Rainbow.*

   Davis's explanation was that, in Haiti, zombies are real. The catch is that they aren't actually dead. He believes that witch doctors produced zombies by dosing victims with tetrodotoxin, the same poison found in puffer fish. The victims fall into a death-like coma, and are subsequently buried alive. The witch doctor returns to the graveyard within hours, before the victim asphyxiates, and digs him up. The victim is then dosed with a powerful hallucinogen called datura, which can cause delirium, mydriasis (severe pupil dilation—that "dead" look), bizarre behavior, and amnesia.

MONOPOLY!

1. The game of Monopoly is descended from a 1903 game called The Landlord's Game. The creator of the game, Lizzie Magie, intended the game to demonstrate that monopolies are bad for society.

2. A Monopoly game comes with $16,280 in Monopoly money. In 1965 a group of fraternity brothers at the University of Delaware were playing a highly publicized marathon game for a fundraiser and ran out of money. They made their own money to continue the game, and were subsequently sued by Parker Brothers for copy right infringement.

3. Special editions of Monopoly were created in 1941 for World War II prisoners of war in hopes to help them escape. Inside the Monopoly game were real money, a file, a compass, and a hidden compartment with a map of the local area with safe houses marked.

1. Fact. Though Parker Brothers rarely acknowledges it, historians have proven that Monopoly is descended from The Landlord's Game. Lizzie Magie was a devout Georgist, which means she believed that land should not be privately owned, but instead belong to all mankind. She wanted her board game to show that rent impoverished tenants and enriched landlords.

2. Bullsh*t! First, the game comes with **$20,580 in Monopoly money**. (This is the same amount as the cash prize in the Monopoly World Championship.)

A marathon game, taking place in **1961** by a group of fraternity brothers at the **University of Pittsburgh**, was stalled when the bank ran out of money. The rules stated that the bank never goes broke, and so the fraternity brothers wired Parker Brothers requesting more money.

Parker Brothers **sent an armored car with $1 million in Monopoly money** to the game so that it could continue.

3. Fact. The British Secret Service approached John Waddington Ltd. (at the time, the manufacturer of Monopoly outside the United States) with the idea. The "special" edition of the game was sent to POW camps by the Red Cross, and some prisoners actually made their escape with the help of the loaded board game.

Fact. Fact. **Bullsh*t!**

OPRAH!

1. *The Oprah Winfrey Show* airs in 145 countries—that's roughly three-quarters of the world. Both CNN and *Time* have said Oprah is the world's most powerful woman. An economic analysis from the University of Maryland suggests that Oprah's endorsement of Barack Obama may have won the 2008 Democratic primary for him.

2. In 1995, Oprah supplanted Bill Cosby as the only African American on the *Forbes* list of the richest 400 people in the country. She was the first black female billionaire in history.

3. The "Oprah effect" describes the postitive influence that Winfrey has on her viewers, particularly in the field of women's health. Winfrey is widely regarded by the medical community as a profoundly helpful source of medical advice for American women.

1. **Fact.** There are 195 countries in the world (give or take, depending on your criteria). *The Oprah Winfrey Show* is distributed in 145 of them, just a hair shy of 75 percent.

Oprah was called "America's most powerful woman" by *Life* magazine, and she was listed as the most powerful celebrity in the world by *Forbes* on multiple occasions.

The Maryland economists estimate that Oprah's endorsement (her first ever since her show debuted in 1986) delivered approximately 1 million popular votes to Obama, enough to flip the outcome in the race between Obama and Hillary Clinton in multiple states. You could argue that she won him the primary, and is subsequently the reason he became president.

That's power.

---

2. **Fact.** In 1995, it was estimated Oprah was worth $340 million. Today, she is worth between $2.5 and $3 **billion** dollars.

In 2000, the University of Illinois offered the course "History 298: Oprah Winfrey, the Tycoon."

---

3. **Bullsh*t!** In general, the "Oprah effect" refers to her ability to increase an author's **book sales** by several orders of magnitude. Sometimes the phrase is used to describe her influence in general, but it does not always have a positive connotation. In fact, Winfrey's selections of "medical" guests and the issues she's championed in the field of women's health have been roundly attacked by scores of medical professionals, and some of them have been called downright "dangerous" for women, including the assumption that childhood vaccines cause autism (no proven link), and the endorsement of injecting hormones into your vagina in order to stay young (dramatically increases the risk of cancer).

Fact. Fact. **Bullsh*t!**

DUNGEONS & DRAGONS!

1. The Waupun Correctional Institution in Wisconsin banned the playing of Dungeons & Dragons by its inmates in 2004, giving the reason that the game could lead to escape fantasies and gang activity.

2. Tiny Hut, Gentle Repose, Touch of Idiocy, Warp Wood, Glibness, and Sepia Snake Sigil are all legitimate spells that magic-using player characters can "cast" in a revised version (3.5) of the "d20 System" Dungeons & Dragons.

3. Action-movie star Vin Diesel suffered the ire of nerds everywhere in 2009 when he publicly referred to Dungeons & Dragons players as "losers." In response to the outcry, the buff actor issued a half-hearted apology on Twitter.

1. **Fact.** When the ban went into effect, "offending" materials were confiscated, such as miniature goblin figurines and dungeon master rule books. The ban was challenged with a lawsuit by a dedicated gamer, Kevin T. Singer, who is serving a life sentence in Waupun. The lawsuit failed, and the prison's decision was upheld. In court, prison officials said they had banned Dungeons & Dragons on the advice of the prison's gang specialist, and that the game could "foster an inmate's obsession with escaping from the real-life correctional environment, fostering hostility, violence, and escape behavior."

2. **Fact.** The "d20 System" is a version of Dungeons & Dragons that relies on twenty-sided dice to determine game action.

    In any role-playing game such as Dungeons & Dragons, players imagine the actions of their characters. While science suggests that such spells cannot be legitimately cast in real life, it is truthful to say that characters can cast them. All the spells mentioned here are listed in the rule book.

3. **Bullsh*t!** That's a cock-and-bull story. Vin Diesel was an **avid Dungeons & Dragons player for over twenty years**, and to this day lights up like a giddy kid when he's asked about his former character "Melkor," a half-Drow witch hunter. Diesel wrote the forward to the book *30 Years of Adventure: A Celebration of Dungeons & Dragons*.

THE WEDGIE!

1. A ten-year-old boy from Grimsby, England, had to undergo emergency surgery to reattach his testicle after he received a wedgie from his classmates.

2. Salt Lake City had to deal with the "Wedgie Bandit" from 2007 to 2009. The Bandit, later identified as Frederick Baze, would pounce on unsuspecting women in public places and yank their underwear before dashing off on foot. He was finally arrested after being caught and pinned to the ground by a local veterinary technician.

3. The Rip Away 1000 is the name of "bully-proof underwear" invented by Jared and Justin Serovich of Columbus, Ohio. As the name suggests, the underwear is designed to tear free if a malicious person yanks on it.

1. **Fact.** The English boy did not blame his friends for his injury, and, in fact, admitted to the media that he himself had been in the habit of doling out wedgies. He underwent an hour-long emergency operation to reattach his testicle to the lining of his scrotum. The boys all admitted to having gotten the idea from seeing wedgies performed on *The Simpsons*.

2. **Bullsh*t!** The Wedgie Bandit doesn't exist, but a law-abiding citizen used a wedgie to good effect: When Salt Lake City thief Frederick Baze tried to steal a car, vet tech Yvonne Miller chased him and managed to stop him by **giving him a wedgie**. After the wedgie, she switched to a headlock and waited for the police.

3. **Fact.** The Rip-Away 1000 is real, and Jared and Justin Serovich really invented it, but I neglected to mention that, at the time, the twin brothers were eight years old. Their invention got them to the finals of a 2007 Ohio invention competition, but it didn't win first prize.

Fact. Fact. **Bullsh*t!**

HARRY POTTER!

1. In one of J. K. Rowling's early outlines for the Harry Potter series, the working title for the first book was *Harry Potter and Bao Zou-long*, referring to the character Harry and his potential sidekick: a talking porcelain doll.

2. The seven Harry Potter volumes make up the bestselling book series of all time, with well over 400 million copies sold. The books have been translated into more than sixty-five languages, including Luxemburgish, Occitan, Faroese, and Ancient Greek.

3. The first Harry Potter film was the 1986 movie *Troll*. In the movie, young Harry Potter is forced to wield a magic staff and battle an evil troll to save his sister, Wendy.

1. **Bullsh*t!** J. K. Rowling never intended to use that title. However, for a time, **you could buy both *Harry Potter and Bao Zoulong* and *Harry Potter and the Porcelain Doll* in China.** The books were quickly recognized as fakes. *Bao Zoulong* primarily featured text lifted from J. R. R. Tolkien's *The Hobbit*, with character names changed to those of Harry Potter characters.

    Similarly, legal pressure convinced an Indian publishing house to stop printing copies of the fraudulent *Harry Potter in Calcutta*.

2. **Fact.** While single-volume books have outsold Harry Potter (the Bible has sold billions upon billions of copies), there is no series of books that have performed as well as J. K. Rowling's stories about the teenage wizard.

    It's hard to imagine that there's much demand for *Harry Potter and the Sorcerer's Stone* in Ancient Greek, but there you have it, they've gone and translated it anyway. (It's called Ἄρειος Ποτὴρ καὶ ἡ τοῦ φιλοσόφου λίθος.)

3. **Fact.** J. K. Rowling claims to have had the idea for a young wizard named Harry Potter in 1990, but a young boy named Harry Potter was already engaging in magical battles in this 1986 cult dark fantasy film. Coincidence? You decide. Harry Potter was played by Noah Hathaway (he was also Atreyu in *The Neverending Story*), and the movie featured a young Julia-Louis Dreyfus. Thanks to Rowling's Potter series, the movie has enjoyed a recent surge in public interest, and a remake is rumored to be in the works.

LOL!

1. Expressions such as "LOL" (an acronym for "laughing out loud") has been proven to be beneficial for e-communication: A study at the University of Tasmania found that using Internet shorthand is twice as efficient for both sender and reader.

2. LOL is an airport in Nevada. Lol is a place in France. Lolol is a town in Chile. "Lol" Tolhurst was the first drummer for the English band The Cure.

3. The French equivalent of "LOL" is "MDR." Coincidentally, *lol* is a real word in both Welsh and Dutch, meaning "nonsense" and "fun," respectively.

1. **Bullsh*t!** First of all, "LOL," like "ROFL," "LMAO," and "BRB," is **not an acronym**. It is an **initialism**. An acronym is pronounced as a word (e.g., "RADAR" or "AIDS"), and an initialism is not (e.g. "FBI" or "NAACP").

   Such initialisms actually **hinder communication**. The University of Tasmania study found that using shorthand, such as "c u ltr b4n" ("See you later. Bye for now."), does save the sender time, but **takes twice as long for the receiver to understand**, even if they are super-tech-savvy texters (like my thirteen-year-old cousin Jenny).

2. **Fact.** The IATA code for Derby Field in Nevada is, in fact, LOL. The very small town of Lol is in Dordogne, France. Lolol is a town in Chile, not far from Santa Cruz.

   There have been several musicians who have gone by "Lol," including Laurence "Lol" Tolhurst of The Cure, the saxophonist Lol Coxhill, and my favorite, the guitarist from the band 10cc, whose name is Lol Creme.

3. **Fact.** "MDR" stands for *mort de rire*, which is an expression that means "laughing," or, more literally, "died of laughter."

   When I learned that *lol* means "nonsense" and "fun" in Welsh and Dutch, I literally laughed out loud.

   LOL!

YOUTUBE!

1. YouTube was founded in 2005 by Chad Hurley, Steve Chen, and Jawed Karim, who had all been employees of PayPal. Google bought YouTube in 2006 for the equivalent of $1.65 billion in Google stock. As of January 2011, YouTube was the third-most-visited site on the Internet, and over thirty-five hours of video were being uploaded to the site *every minute.*

2. The first video ever uploaded to YouTube was called "Roundhay Garden Scene." It depicted four people walking around in a garden, and it was only two seconds long.

3. A company called Universal Tube & Rollform Equipment filed a lawsuit against YouTube in 2006 because its website, utube.com, was getting bombarded by so much Internet traffic that its servers crashed.

1. **Fact.** The website youtube.com ranks third after google.com and facebook.com. The site paypal.com ranks thirty-second, and, just in case you were wondering (I was), taco.com ranks around 3,162,932nd.

   Thirty-five hours of video content per minute means that it would take you five and three-quarters years of watching nonstop in order to see everything that is uploaded to YouTube in one day.

2. **Bullsh*t!** The first video was uploaded to YouTube on April 23, 2005. Still on the site, it is called **"Me at the Zoo"** and features YouTube founder Jawed Karim at the San Diego Zoo.

   Roundhay Garden Scene is the name of the earliest surviving motion picture ever recorded. Filmed in 1888 at 12 frames per second, it is indeed two seconds long and depicts four people walking around in a garden.

3. **Fact.** YouTube and Universal Tube settled their dispute in 2007. Universal Tube now hosts ads on the site utube.com, which presumably adds quite a bit of revenue to its coffers.

BUGS BUNNY!

1. Bugs Bunny got his name from a 1945 Brooklyn Heights ferryboat that several animators took on a daily basis. Brooklyn Heights had the nickname "Bugtown," often shortened to "Bugs," and the three local ferries were known colloquially as *Bugs Bunny*, *Bugs Blimpie*, and *Bugs Boxcar*.

---

2. From the character's inception to 1989, Bugs Bunny was voiced by Mel Blanc. Blanc was also the voice of Daffy Duck, Porky Pig, and Barney Rubble from *The Flintstones*.

---

3. "Mutiny on the Bunny," "Water, Water Every Hare," "Hare and Loathing in Las Vegas," "Hare-Abian Nights," and "People Are Bunny" are all real Bugs Bunny cartoons.

1. **Bullsh*t!** I totally made all of that up.

Bugs Bunny got his name from **Ben "Bugs" Hardaway**, who was an animator and storyboard artist during animation's golden years. He drew an initial sketch of the rascally rabbit, and other members of the studio referred to it as **Bugs's Bunny** as it was passed around. The name stuck, and the possessive 's was eventually dropped.

The first incarnation of Bugs Bunny appeared, nameless, in the cartoon *Porky's Hare Hunt* in 1938.

2. **Fact.** Known as the "man of a thousand voices," Blanc was indeed the voice of Bugs, Daffy, Porky, and Barney, not to mention Tweety Bird, Mr. Spacely (from *The Jetsons*), Captain Caveman, Speedy Gonzalez, Sylvester the Cat, Foghorn Leghorn, Yosemite Sam, Pepé Le Pew, and Wile E. Coyote.

3. **Fact.** They are, and so are "Apes of Wrath," "Hare-Way to the Stars," "Now Hare This," and "A-Lad-In His Lamp."

THE MOUSTACHE!

1. The longest moustache ever recorded belonged to Badamsinh Juwansinh Gurjar of India. It was measured in 2004 to be a mind-boggling 12½ feet long.

2. The Fu Manchu was named after Ching-kuo Manchu (whose nickname among the American military was "Fu Manchu," meaning "Lord Manchu"), the chairman of Nationalist China from 1928 to 1931, who sported a substantial beard.

3. Every two years, a different city hosts the World Beard and Moustache Championships, which feature delightful competitions in diverse categories such as "Hungarian moustache," "Dali moustache," and "freestyle full beard." Historically, Team Germany has been dominant, but Team USA has recently been taking titles.

1. **Fact.** Gurjar's mighty moustache earned him a Guinness World Record.

   Currently, the longest moustache belongs to Ram Singh Chauhan, also of India, and measures 11½ feet long.

2. **Bullsh*t!** The Fu Manchu moustache was named after Fu Manchu, a **fictional character**. He was invented by British author Sax Rohmer for a series of novels in the first half of the twentieth century, including *The Mask of Fu Manchu* and *The Island of Fu Manchu*. The character went on to be immortalized in film and popular culture. Fu Manchu was a despicable villain of the highest order, and has long been controversial, with many critics arguing that he represented a racist Chinese stereotype.

   The chairman of Nationalist China from 1928 to 1931 was **Chiang Kai-shek**, a clean-shaven man.

3. **Fact.** The competition began in the early '90s in southwestern Germany. With the advent of the Internet, the championships grew each year. Typically, the event is held in Europe, but the 2009 competition took place in Anchorage, Alaska, and Team USA won a number of events. These days the WBMC is the self-described "premiere event in the sport of bearding."

Fact. Fact. **Bullsh*t!**

SUPERMAN!

1. When the character of Superman was first conceived by Jerry Siegel in 1933, he was a vagrant named Bill Dunn who is given telepathic powers by a mad scientist. This Superman was an evil, bald, ruthless villain.

---

2. Superman in his now-ubiquitous hero form first appeared in *Action Comics #1* in 1938. The cover featured Superman lifting a car over his head. In 2010 a copy of *Action Comics #1* in good condition sold on the Internet for $1 million.

---

3. The first feature film to star Superman was 1982's *Superman: The Movie*, starring Christopher Reeve as the Man of Steel.

1. **Fact.** Jerry Siegel first published a short story called "The Reign of the Super-Man" about the power-hungry Dunn, which was inspired by Friedrich Nietzsche's ideas of the Übermensch, which is often translated as the "above-human," the "overman," or the "super-man." The story was illustrated by Joe Shuster, and Shuster and Siegel would go on to recast Superman as the hero we know today.

The villain Lex Luthor bears a lot of similarities to this original idea of Superman.

2. **Fact.** As of 2010, there were only about 100 copies of *Action Comics #1* in existence, and most of those were not in good condition. The copy in question had a quality rating of 8 out of 10, which means it was in "very fine" condition.

A million dollars might sound like a crazy price for a silly comic book, but some experts believe it's actually a good investment. With so few copies in existence, the value should continue to rise.

Some diehard Superman fans think the comic book belongs in a museum.

3. **Bullsh*t!** *Superman: The Movie* came out in **1978**, and was the **second** feature film about Superman. The first was the black-and-white 1951 movie ***Superman and the Mole-Men***, which starred George Reeves as the superhero from Krypton.

SUPERCALIFRAGILISTIC-
EXPIALIDOCIOUS!

1. "Supercalifragilisticexpialidocious" is the longest word in the English language to appear in major dictionaries during the past several decades.

2. There were versions of the word "supercalifragilisticexpialidocious" in popular culture before it appeared in the 1964 movie *Mary Poppins* as a song title. Gloria Parker and Barney Young wrote a song in 1951 called "Supercalafajalistickespeealadojus." The writers of the *Mary Poppins* song stated they heard a version of the word while boys at summer camp and that it was phrased "super-cadja-flawjalistic-espealedojus."

3. Dutch finger-style guitarist Eltjo Haselhoff recorded a solo acoustic guitar version of the *Mary Poppins* song "Supercalifragilisticexpialidocious" for the 2009 album *Poppin' Guitars: A Tuneful of Sherman*. The album also features the songs "Chim Chim Cher-ee," "Chitty Chitty Bang Bang," and "Let's Get Together."

1. **Bullsh*t!** The word, at thirty-four letters in length, has appeared in most major dictionaries, and came awfully close to being the longest. It has been beaten regularly, however, by the thirty-five-letter word "Hippopotomonstrosesquipedaliophobia," which means **the fear of long words**.

   Scientific and technical words can get very long: The forty-five-letter word "pneumonoultramicroscopicsilicovolcanoconiosis," which describes a lung condition, is the longest word to appear in major dictionaries over the last few decades.

2. **Fact.** Parker and Young actually filed a copyright-infringement suit against Wonderland Music, the publisher of the "Supercalifragilisticexpialidocious" song from *Mary Poppins*, but they were not successful. The judge ruled in favor of Wonderland because it was proven in court that many variants of the word were known prior to either song's publication.

   Brothers Richard and Robert Sherman, who wrote the song for the Disney movie, stated that they learned a version of the word while at summer camp in the Adirondacks in the 1930s.

---

3. **Fact.** Eltjo Haselhoff was one of several artists who recorded songs for the album. Australian guitarist Nick Charles recorded "Chim Chim Cher-ee," also from *Mary Poppins*. Mark Hanson recorded "Chitty Chitty Bang Bang" from the movie *Chitty Chitty Bang Bang*, and *Prairie Home Companion* guitarist Pat Donohue recorded "Let's Get Together" from *The Parent Trap*. (Not to be confused with *Let's Stay Together* by Al Green, which would be quite out of place on this album.)

THE IPOD!

1. The iPod got its name from a freelance copywriter named Vinnie Chieco, whose inspiration was the sci-fi movie *2001: A Space Odyssey*. The iPod launched in 2001.

2. All iPods are manufactured in the U.S. in Cary, North Carolina, by ProFox Industries. ProFox is purported to be one of the best companies to work for in the United States, with on-site healthcare, childcare, and a 66,000-square-foot gym.

3. Apple has sold about as many iPods as there are people in the United States.

1. **Fact.** When Chieco caught his first glimpse of the white iPod, he thought of pods connecting to a spaceship, and recalled the line from *2001*: "Open the pod bay door, Hal!"

   The 2001 launch was not, however, the first time the consumer world had encountered a product of that name. "IPOD" was first trademarked in 1991 for office furniture by the Chrysalis Corporation. It was trademarked by two separate companies for two kinds of software in 1999, and it was trademarked for Internet kiosks in 2000.

   Now Apple holds all the rights to the word "iPod."

2. **Bullsh*t!** Our iPods, iPhones, and iPads are manufactured **in Taiwan** by a company called **Foxconn**. Foxconn is constantly mired in controversy due to allegations of **horrible working conditions**. In 2010 alone, **eighteen Foxconn workers attempted suicide**.

   Cary is not home to a company named ProFox, but software maker SAS is headquartered there. Employees of SAS enjoy on-site healthcare and childcare, a 66,000-square-foot gym, a beauty salon, and car cleaning. *Fortune* named SAS number one on its "100 Best Companies to Work For" list for two years running.

3. **Fact.** There are 308 million people in the United States, give or take a million, and Apple has sold more than 300 million iPods to date.

JAZZ!

1. The word "jazz" comes from the Swahili word *juzi*, which means "dream."

---

2. Jazz historians generally agree that the first jazz record ever made was "Livery Stable Blues" from the Original Dixieland Jass Band. The record came out in 1917, and included the title song as well as "Dixie Jass Band One-Step."

---

3. Jelly Roll Morton, born in 1885, claimed to have invented jazz. Some of his famous jazz recordings include "Black Bottom Stomp," "Burnin' the Iceberg," "Red Hot Pepper," "Frookish," and "Creepy Feeling."

1. **Bullsh*t!** The Swahili word *juzi* means **"the day before yester-day,"** and the Swahili word for "dream" is **ndoto**. Jazz can trace its roots to the arrival of African slaves in the United States, but few of them would have spoken Swahili, since it is from East Africa, and the American slave trade primarily preyed on West Africa.

   The exact etymology of the word "jazz" remains **unknown**. By 1912 the word was in use as slang, though not necessarily in reference to music. By 1915 the word was being used to describe Chicago music.

2. **Fact.** The 1917 single was the first major recording of music that referred to itself as jazz (or "jass," in this case) and arguably the first jazz record. Ragtime and blues, genres that are part of jazz history but generally regarded as separate from jazz, had already been recorded extensively.

   The Original Dixieland Jass Band was entirely made up of white musicians.

3. **Fact.** Ferdinand Joseph LaMothe was born into a Creole community in New Orleans in 1885. During his childhood he became a highly skilled ragtime pianist, and at age fourteen he took a job playing piano in a brothel. It was there that he took on the stage name Jelly Roll Morton, "jelly roll" being a slang term at the time for female genitalia.

   He was notorious for his larger-than-life persona and his frequent assertions that he invented jazz.

Fact. Fact. **Bullsh*t!**

CHAPTER 3

Everything
Edible

I remember learning about the four basic food groups in elementary school. It was so simple, even a third grader could understand it: Just eat equal parts meat, fruits/vegetables, grains, and milk, and you're certifiably healthy. Except that it was total bullshit.

I'm a proud former Texan, a meat-lover, and a master at the grill, but even I recognize that as long as you're protein-conscious, meat is far from mandatory. I love ice cream as much as the next guy, but dairy is not, and has never been, an essential part of a healthy diet. In fact, most people in the world are lactose-intolerant to some degree.

Were we in the dark ages in the '80s and '90s when we believed that meat and milk should account for *half* of our diets? No. As it turns out, scientists never truly believed that. While creating the four basic food groups, the USDA was heavily influenced by America's cattle ranchers and dairy farmers and their powerful lobbies. I love our ranchers and farmers, but it's probably not a good policy to take nutrition advice from the people selling the food.

Do you know more than the next guy about the food we eat? Turn the page and find out.

COCA-COLA!

1. "The World's Most Delicious Drink," "More Bounce to the Ounce," "Gotta Have It," and "Be Sociable" were all Coca-Cola slogans at one time.

2. The first formula of Coca-Cola, called Pemberton's French Wine Coca, was alcoholic and meant to be medicine.

3. Coca-Cola sells more than 3,000 different products in more than 200 countries. Minute Maid, Glacéau (VitaminWater), Powerade, Odwalla, Nestea, Hi-C, Mr. Pibb, and Dasani are all Coca-Cola brands. Lesser known Coca Cola brands include Jaz Cola, Love Body, and Water Salad.

1. **Bullsh*t!** Those were all **Pepsi slogans**.

    Some of my favorite Coca-Cola slogans are "It Had to Be Good to Get Where It Is," "The Pause That Refreshes," and "Enjoy." But the best one from all time is the Coca-Cola slogan from 1906: "The Great National Temperance Beverage."

2. **Fact.** Pharmacist John Pemberton created the medicinal tonic in the late nineteenth century. Not only was it alcoholic, but it also included **cocaine** as a major ingredient. At the time, cocaine was used as a medicine frequently, and its harmful and highly addictive qualities were not yet popularly known. By the time he called it Coca-Cola, Pemberton had removed alcohol from the recipe but **kept the cocaine**.

    Over the years, as the recipe was refined, and cocaine became vilified, the amount was reduced bit by bit, until it only had the merest trace. The beverage was cocaine-free by 1929.

    Coca-Cola still contains specially prepared cocaine-free extracts of the coca leaf. The extracted cocaine is sold for "medicinal" purposes.

---

3. **Fact.** Coca-Cola is all over the globe in thousands of permutations.

    Jaz Cola is specifically marketed to the Philippines. Love Body is a tea drink in Japan that is supposed to be good for women's health. Water Salad is also marketed in Japan.

    Personally, I think Water Salad would do well here in the States.

THE TOMATO!

1. Tomatoes are members of the genus *Solanum*, which also includes potatoes and eggplants. They are in the family Solanaceae, which includes chili peppers, tobacco, and petunias. Most parts of most of the plants in *Solanum* and Solanaceae are poisonous to humans.

---

2. In the 1973 case *Nix v. Hedden*, the Supreme Court was charged with the task of determining whether the tomato was a fruit or a vegetable. It sided with the botanist, Murphy Nix, declaring the tomato to be officially a fruit.

---

3. The first ever genetically modified food crop to be successfully commercialized and brought to market was a biotechnology-produced kind of tomato called the Flavr Savr.

1. **Fact.** The Solanaceae family is informally known as the nightshade family. *Atropa belladonna*, or deadly nightshade, is part of the family.

   Plants in Solanaceae and *Solanum* are generally rich in alkaloids, which in some cases can be desirable nutritionally, and in others can be downright fatal. The green parts of a tomato plant contain the alkaloid tomatine, which is toxic to humans.

2. **Bullsh*t!** *Nix v. Hedden* did occur, although in **1893**, and the Supreme Court was indeed asked to decide whether the tomato was a fruit or a vegetable. The ruling, however, was that the tomato is a **vegetable**.

   The case occurred because of a nineteenth-century law that required tax to be paid on imported vegetables, but not fruit. The Supreme Court acknowledged that, in botanical terms, tomatoes are **fruits**, but decided that tomatoes are vegetables based on their typical use and popular perception. (Our country has a long history of major branches of government ignoring science.)

3. **Fact.** Scientifically, the Flavr Savr was a success. Researchers at Calgene Inc. managed to introduce an inhibitor to tomatoes that would prevent them from producing the enzyme that causes the fruit to soften over time. The resultant tomatoes, Flavr Savr tomatoes, stayed firm for much longer, and were available in supermarkets in the U.S. in the early '90s.

   Commercially, Flavr Savrs didn't last. It seems the expense of producing them and the growing public sentiment against genetically modified foods were insurmountable hurdles.

RICE!

1. California is the U.S.'s leading producer of rice. In 2008, the state churned out over 800 million pounds of rice. Second and third place go to Florida and Texas, respectively.

---

2. Colorado-based Ventria Bioscience has genetically modified rice to contain proteins normally found in breast milk. The resultant rice boosts the immune system.

---

3. Despite the urban legend stating the contrary, throwing uncooked rice at weddings is not dangerous to birds at all.

1. **Bullsh*t!** The U.S.'s leading producer of rice is **Arkansas**, by a landslide, which produces more than **9 billion pounds** of rice each year.

   California does take second place, although it's far behind the Natural State, producing 4 billion pounds of rice each year.

   Third, fourth, and fifth place go to Louisiana, Mississippi, and Missouri, respectively. Texas is sixth, and Florida seventh, each producing less than a billion pounds a year each.

2. **Fact.** Ventria's rice contains the proteins lactoferrin and lysozyme, which are both found in human breast milk. (Lactoferrin also occurs naturally in cow's milk, and lysozyme in egg whites.) Both proteins are active in fighting bacteria.

   The special rice is used in a hydrating solution for children in developing countries. The solution helps them stave off diarrhea and bacterial infection, problems that are easily treated with modern medicine, but nevertheless contribute to the deaths of millions of children each year.

3. **Fact.** If I had a nickel for every time somebody informed me that instant rice absorbs the moisture inside a bird's stomach, expands, and causes the bird to burst, I could buy a gumball or two.

   The myth has been popular for decades now, and many wedding parties opt to throw birdseed or blow bubbles instead. Birds are quite content to eat your uncooked rice, however, and begin to digest it long before it can swell to outrageous proportions.

Fact. Fact. **Bullsh*t!**

FRENCH FRIES!

1. French fries got their start in seventeenth-century France. Initially twice-fried in expensive oil, *pommes frites* were the province of the wealthy elite for nearly a century before they began to gain popularity throughout the world.

---

2. French fries are the single most popular fast food item in the United States. Nutrition experts estimate that ¼ of the vegetables consumed by children in the U.S. are in the form of either potato chips or French fries. In 2004, U.S. citizens put away 7.5 billion pounds of frozen French fries.

---

3. When it was revealed in 1990 that McDonald's used beef tallow in the preparation of its French fries, Hindu vegetarians in Bombay, India, ransacked a local store and smeared cow dung all over the statue of Ronald McDonald inside.

1. **Bullsh*t!** "French" fries began in the Spanish Netherlands, now modern **Belgium**. Poor villagers in the Meuse valley were accustomed to frying fish to accompany their meals. In 1680, there was a shortage of fish, and villagers substituted thinly cut potatoes. The dish quickly caught on throughout Europe. The rest of the world—even the French—concede that French fries come from Belgium.

   To this day, fries are more popular in Belgium than anywhere else, even the United States!

2. **Fact.** We are simply obsessed with our fried potatoes. French fries account for ¼ of an average child's vegetable intake—and that percentage jumps to ⅓ once those children become teenagers. Of the 7.5 billion pounds of frozen French fries we consumed in 2004, 90 percent were sold by fast food outlets.

---

3. **Fact.** Word initially spread in 1989 that McDonald's was using beef tallow in the preparation of its fries, which distressed many vegetarians. In 1990, the company proudly announced that it had switched to vegetable oil, but it was later disclosed that beef tallow was still included in the flavorings. The resultant uproar led to the Indian case of vandalism. McDonald's denied that beef tallow was used in fry preparation in India.

   Some Americans sued McDonald's for falsely claiming that the fries were vegetarian. McDonald's settled out of court, posting an apology on its website and paying $10 million to vegetarian groups and to the twelve individuals involved in the suit.

   Still, McDonald's denied ever claiming that the fries were vegetarian.

MARSHMALLOWS!

1. Marshmallow sweets date back to ancient Egypt, where the sap of the marsh mallow plant was combined with honey and nuts to make a luxury confection. In medieval Europe, marshmallow sap was used as a cure for a sore throat.

2. When modern marshmallows were invented in France, extract from the *Althaea officinalis* plant was whipped up to create the gooey treat. Today, none of the major United States marshmallow makers use the plant *at all* to make marshmallows.

3. When high school senior Brittany Garcia walked away with only minor injuries after being hit by a car in October 2010, doctors proclaimed that marshmallows might have saved her life. The Halloween bunny costume she wore that day was made of thousands of the little white treats.

1. **Fact.** Those Egyptians had it right. Time to convince your history professor that you need to re-create the practice. You know, for your studies.

   And who are we to say that marshmallows don't cure a sore throat? I'm saving a bag for the next time I get the flu.

---

2. **Fact.** Marshmallows get their name from the marsh mallow (scientific name *Althaea officinalis*), a pink-flowered plant that, naturally, grows in marshes. There are other kinds of mallow, including musk mallow, tree mallow, and Indian mallow. Marshmallow sap is sweet.

   Big-brand marshmallows in stores are made from primarily corn syrup, starch, sugar, water, and, in place of marshmallow extract, gelatin. I propose we change the official name to Corny Gelatin Sugar Bombs.

   It's likely that you (and I) have never tasted real marshmallow.

3. **Bullsh*t!** That's ridiculous. Who makes a bunny costume out of marshmallows?

   In reality, **marshmallows kill**. At least two people have died playing the game Chubby Bunny, which involves stuffing your mouth with as many marshmallows as possible, including a twelve-year-old girl who suffocated to death while playing the game at a school fair.

BEER!

1. Beer is mostly water. Because of this, the type of water used in the beer-making process has a significant effect on the taste of the beer. Dublin's hard water is most suitable for stouts, while Pilsen's soft water is best for pale lagers.

2. According to annual Gallup polls, about 78 percent of U.S. adults "have occasion to use alcoholic beverages." When it comes to beverage of choice, it has been nearly a dead heat between wine and beer since the mid-1940s, with wine slightly edging ahead of beer each year. Beer took the lead only once, in 2005.

3. A program was launched in Belgium in 2001 to replace sugary drinks and soda in school lunchrooms with a healthier option: beer. Students had the option between lager and bitter, and 80 percent of the children in the pilot programs said they enjoyed having beer with lunch.

1. **Fact.** Typical ingredients of beer are water (mostly), a fermented starch, yeast, and a flavoring, such as hops.

   The mineral content of the water used does have an effect on the taste of the beer. Hard water, high in minerals such as calcium and sulfate, enhances bitterness. Soft water, free of most minerals, has a cleaner taste.

   This is likely why Guinness brewed in Dublin tastes different from Guinness brewed in London.

2. **Bullsh*t!** Actually, the reverse is true when it comes to alcoholic beverage preference. Beer has maintained the lead each year, with wine nipping at its heels. The exception is 2005, when wine took the top honors by three percentage points. Hard liquor is fairly distant in third place.

   We're also a little dryer than stated: Gallup reports that only **64 percent of U.S. adults drink alcohol occasionally**, and it has been that way since the mid-1940s, with a brief increase during the 1970s (up to 71 percent).

3. **Fact.** Rony Langenaeken, the chairman of De Limburgse Biervrienden, the beer club behind the plan, was quoted as saying: "Beer is for the whole family." The program was drawn out for students ages three to fifteen.

   A special beer was used for the pilot programs, called *tafelbier*, which contained no more than 2.5 percent alcohol.

SLICED BREAD!

1. The first loaf-at-a-time bread-slicing machine was invented in 1888 in Schenectady, New York, by a machinist named Cornell Woolridge. Packaging and selling sliced bread would not become a popular nationwide practice until 1937, however, and Woolridge never made a single penny from his invention.

2. A bakery in Chillicothe, Missouri, was the first to sell presliced bread. They called it Kleen Maid Bread and marketed as "the greatest forward step in the baking industry since bread was wrapped." From this, the phrase "the greatest thing since sliced bread" is thought to have originated.

3. Selling sliced bread was banned by the U.S. government in 1943 at the height of World War II. The order was given by Claude R. Wickard, the secretary of agriculture at the time. The ban was supposed to help conserve wax paper (which was needed to keep sliced bread fresh) and to bring the cost of bread down.

1. **Bullsh*t!** The first loaf-at-a-time bread-slicing machine was invented in **1928** by a **jeweler** named **Otto Rohwedder** of **Davenport, Iowa**. It was an immediate hit. In **1930**, the Continental Baking Company introduced presliced **Wonder Bread**, using machines that were improved versions of Rohwedder's design. Rohwedder sold the machines for two decades before retiring.

2. **Fact.** The Chillicothe Baking Company bought Rohwedder's first automatic bread-slicer in 1928 and put it to work. On July 7, 1928, a prophetic columnist wrote in the *Chillicothe Constitution-Tribune*: "So neat and precise are the slices . . . that one realizes instantly that here is a refinement that will receive a hearty and permanent welcome."

3. **Fact.** It turns out that most major bakeries had huge stores of wax paper already, and the ban did not decrease the price of bread. Most importantly, the ban was hugely unpopular. A letter from a frustrated homemaker appeared in the *New York Times* on January 26, 1943:

   "I should like to let you know how important sliced bread is to the morale and saneness of a household. My husband and four children are all in a rush during and after breakfast. Without ready-sliced bread I must do the slicing for toast—two pieces for each one—that's ten. For their lunches I must cut by hand at least twenty slices, for two sandwiches apiece. Afterward I make my own toast. Twenty-two slices of bread to be cut in a hurry!"

   The ban was lifted on March 8, 1943, less than two months after it was introduced.

HIGH-FRUCTOSE CORN SYRUP!

1. High-fructose corn syrup is made by soaking and fermenting corn kernels to extract cornstarch, then using enzymes to turn the glucose in the starch into fructose. It is a primary sweetener in American processed foods because it is cheaper than sugar. Many studies have suggested that high-fructose corn syrup is more harmful to the body than cane sugar.

2. The average U.S. citizen consumes more than 40 pounds of high-fructose corn syrup each year, and well over a hundred pounds of sweeteners in general (including sugar)

3. In a 2011 study at Wesleyan University, trace amounts of toxic chemicals were found in samples of the high-fructose corn syrup used by major American food companies, including ammonia, formaldehyde, and acetone.

1. **Fact.** Corn syrup is cheaper in the United States thanks to long-running heavy government subsidies on corn. Add to that a stiff import tax on sugar, and it's no wonder why major food companies sweeten with syrup. The stuff also stores better, doesn't mask flavors like regular sugar, has a lower freezing point, and retains moisture well.

   There is still plenty of controversy as to whether there is a significant nutritional difference between table sugar (made from sugar cane or sugar beets and primarily sucrose) and high-fructose corn syrup, but many studies suggest that it contributes to the obesity epidemic.

---

2. **Fact.** The United States Department of Agriculture's Economic Research Service calculates the per capita availability of sweeteners in the U.S. by year. The numbers can't tell us *exactly* how much high-fructose corn syrup each person consumes, but they do reflect the buying habits of the consumer.

   Since 1985, the per capita availability has been well over 40 pounds. We may be consuming as much as 50 pounds per year of the gooey stuff, and 130 pounds of sugar. And remember, that's *on average*, meaning there's a hefty squad of people out there who are consuming more.

3. **Bullsh*t!** High-fructose corn syrup may be bad for you, but it's not *that* bad. You can find those chemicals, however, in **cigarettes** and cigarette smoke, along with cyanide and carbon monoxide.

   It is true, however, that high-fructose corn syrup is sometimes made with **hydrochloric acid**.

BACON!

1. The bacon we typically eat in the United States is back meat from a pig that has been smoked and cured. The word "bacon" comes from the Latin *bacca*, which means, appropriately, "back."

2. In 2009, chefs and students at Lock Haven University used 225 pounds of bacon to construct a 203-foot-long BLT sandwich.

3. The American company J&D's offers bacon-flavored envelopes. The delicious mailers have bacon flavoring in the glue, so that you can taste bacon every time you send a letter. The products are marketed under the name Mmmvelopes.

1. **Bullsh*t!** Pork loin and fatback, both from the back of the pig, are popular kinds of bacon in other countries. The bacon most Americans eat comes from the **underside** of the pig, or **pork belly**. In fact, the USDA defines bacon as the "cured belly of a swine carcass." *Mmmmmmm.*

   Bacon is cured but not necessarily smoked before we buy it. Smoking it is just one of many glorious options we enjoy when it comes to bacon preparation.

   The word bacon actually comes from the **Old High German** *bahho*, which meant either "bacon" or "buttock." Since their bacon likely came from the back and buttocks of the pig, it probably meant both! *Bacca* is a kind of fruit.

2. **Fact.** The mighty sandwich, which also featured 200 pounds of tomatoes and 165 pounds of lettuce, was undertaken to beat the previous world record of 179 feet. Lock Haven students did not waste time admiring their creation: The massive BLT was consumed immediately.

3. **Fact.** J&D's company slogan is "Everything Should Taste Like Bacon."

   J&D's is also popular for its Bacon Salt and its bacon-flavored mayonnaise, Baconnaise.

PEPPER!

1. The black pepper on the tables of your neighborhood restaurant is the ground, dried fruit of the *Piper nigrum* plant, which is a perennial flowering woody vine. The plant is native to India, but the world's largest cultivator of *Piper nigrum* is Vietnam.

2. Although it is now one of the most common spices in the world, black pepper was once so valuable that it was used as currency.

3. The Egyptian pharaoh Ramesses II used black pepper as a means of torture: On his orders, victims *had their orifices stuffed* with hundreds of little black peppercorns.

1. **Fact.** *Piper nigrum* is indeed the scientific name of the black pepper plant. Peppercorns are, scientifically, fruits.

   Black pepper is a perennial flowering woody vine because it lives for longer than two years, it produces flowers, its stems are made of wood, and it is a climbing plant.

   Piper nigrum is native to India, but it is a major crop in Vietnam, which produces a third of the world's black pepper.

   ---

2. **Fact.** Throughout most of history, the vast majority of black pepper came from India. The spice was in great demand, and those who could control the spice trade gained a huge economic advantage.

   Pepper was highly coveted in ancient Greece and Rome, and in medieval Europe it was sometimes used as collateral or currency. The Dutch word *peperduur*, meaning "expensive as pepper," is still in use today.

   Desire for an overseas black pepper trade route to India was a major motivation for the Portuguese to conduct their major exploratory sea voyages, which spawned the Age of Discovery.

3. **Bullsh*t!** That's ridiculous. It's supremely unlikely that Ramesses II ever ordered someone stuffed with black pepper.

   However, the **mummy of Ramesses II** was discovered with black peppercorns in its abdomen, and **peppercorns packed inside its nose**. Egyptologists have been baffled by this, since it is not common. One benefit Ramesses II enjoys because of his pepper-lined nose is a decent profile: Most mummies have flattened noses thanks to the wrapping process, but Ramesses II still has a distinct, hook-shaped nose.

WATERMELON!

1. The watermelon is the official state fruit of Oklahoma. Scientifically speaking, the watermelon is also a kind of nut.

---

2. The National Watermelon Association annually crowns a Watermelon Queen. The queen is selected in a pageant "with focus on speech and interview" skills.

---

3. An old Romani legend from the Balkans maintained that a watermelon left alone for too long could turn into a vampire. Vampire watermelons were thought to growl, roll around, and thirst for blood.

1. **Bullsh*t!** In 2007, Oklahoma named the watermelon its **official state vegetable**. The watermelon is definitely a fruit, not a vegetable, though it is in the family Cucurbitaceae, which includes squash, pumpkin, and zucchini, **all of which, scientifically, are fruits**. Why does Oklahoma call the watermelon a vegetable? They already had a state fruit—the strawberry.

    Watermelons are not nuts at all. But they are, technically, **berries**. A berry is a fleshy fruit derived from a single ovary. Watermelons are also **pepos**, which are berries with hard rinds.

2. **Fact.** The lucky lady is crowned each year at the National Watermelon Association Convention.

3. **Fact.** It is an actual, documented legend, although there is some debate as to whether this was a serious belief or a funny story passed down through generations in the style of fairy tales.

    Tatomir P. Vukanović, a Balkan historian, wrote about the legend in an article for the *Journal of the Gypsy Lore Society*: "Vampires of ground fruit origin are believed to have the same shape and appearance as the original plant. . . . [They] go round the houses, stables, and rooms at night, all by themselves, and do harm to people. But it is thought that they cannot do great damage to folk, so people are not very afraid of this kind of vampire."

    Next time you have a slice of watermelon, consider yourself a hero for preventing a vampire attack.

CHEESE!

1. Our seventh president, Andrew Jackson, was known for throwing White House parties that were open to the public. At his last party, President Jackson served a 3-foot-high, 4-foot-diameter, 1,400-pound wheel of cheddar, which was consumed by guests in two hours.

2. Velveeta, Easy Cheese (in a spray can), and the square American Kraft Singles are *not* cheeses, and contain no real cheese at all. All three are made of soy protein concentrate.

3. A study by the British Cheese Board concluded that eating a piece of cheese before sleep produced vivid dreams. The results indicated that different types of cheese produce different types of dreams.

1. **Fact.** The enormous wheel of cheese was a gift, and Jackson reportedly let it age for two years in the White House lobby. He offered it to guests during his last party, and they consumed it immediately, which, if you ask me, was their patriotic duty.

Historians note that the lobby was left with numerous cheese stains, and that it smelled like cheese for weeks.

2. **Bullsh*t!** Velveeta, Easy Cheese, and American Kraft Singles are all **made with real cheese**, but Kraft, which makes all three products, cannot legally call them cheese because of rules dictated by the Food and Drug Administration. In truth, they are **processed cheese**, which is cheese that has various ingredients added, such as emulsifiers, whey, unfermented milk products (like cream), salt, and food coloring.

That fancy herbed Brie you find at the store has ingredients added (little green herb flecks), but the FDA doesn't require it to be labeled "pasteurized prepared cheese product."

Sounds like a double standard to me!

3. **Fact.** Wacky but true. The British Cheese Board's goal for the study was to determine whether eating cheese before bed leads to nightmares, as a popular myth claims.

The study's volunteers reported few nightmares, but most reported vivid dreams. Researchers noticed a link between types of dreams and the type of cheese consumed.

Volunteers who ate cheddar seemed to dream about celebrities, while those who consumed Red Leicester had nostalgic dreams. Volunteers who sampled Lancashire dreamed about work, while those who ate blue cheese reported very vivid, bizarre dreams.

Fact. Fact. **Bullsh*t!**

THE SANDWICH!

1. The Sandwich Islands, an equatorial volcanic archipelago in the Pacific 500 miles west of Ecuador, were named by British explorer Edward Teach after his patron, John Capulet, the forty-seventh Earl of Sandwich. The sandwich was invented by Capulet.

2. In 2006 a Massachusetts state senator, Jarrett Barrios, threatened legislation to restrict schools from serving Fluffernutter sandwiches more than once a week to children. The measure caused a major uproar from his constituents and even other politicians, including a state representative, Kathi-Anne Reinstein, who promised to file legislation that would make the Fluffernutter the official sandwich of Massachusetts.

3. According to a court ruling in Boston, a sandwich must include "at least two slices of bread." The court ruling went on to state that burritos, quesadillas, and tacos are therefore not sandwiches.

1. **Bullsh*t!** The islands 500 miles west of Ecuador are not the Sandwich Islands—they are called the **Galápagos Islands**. The "Sandwich Islands" was the first name given to a different Pacific archipelago—which we know as **Hawaii**. The explorer **James Cook** (not Edward Teach, who was the pirate **Blackbeard**) named the Hawaiian Islands the Sandwich Islands after **John Montague, the fourth Earl of Sandwich**. Montague, an industrious man, used to insist on his lunch arriving between two pieces of bread so that he could continue to work.

   It is said that others would order their meat "the same as Sandwich!" and the term was born.

2. **Fact.** In case you've been living under a rock, a Fluffernutter is a white-bread sandwich with a layer of peanut butter and a layer of marshmallow cream.

   Senator Barrios was understandably reacting to the low nutritional value of the sandwich his son Nathaniel had been given at school, but he failed to properly assess the public opinion in Massachusetts of the decadent treat. (Marshmallow Fluff was invented in Somerville, Massachusetts.)

   In response to the furor, Barrios abandoned his mission, and Representative Reinstein retracted hers as well.

3. **Fact.** The court made the ruling after Panera Bread filed a complaint that its no-compete clause in a shopping center was violated by the introduction of a Qdoba Mexican Grill. Since Panera produces sandwiches, and Qdoba produces burritos, the court found that there was, in fact, no competition going on.

TEQUILA!

1. A bottle of tequila sold in 1996 for $225,000, earning it the Guinness World Record for most expensive bottle of spirits ever sold. The same company is eager to break its own record, and in 2010 unveiled a bottle of tequila on sale for $3.5 million.

2. When mescal and tequila were first produced in Mexico, it was traditional for the bottle to have a worm at the bottom, which was (ick!) seen as a seal of quality. Nowadays, export bottles rarely have worms in them because of negative public perception, but the worms are still very much present in true Mexican tequila.

3. Tequila is not just a drink—it's a scientific marvel. Physicists from the National Autonomous University of Mexico recently discovered how to make diamonds out of tequila.

1. **Fact.** Distiller Hacienda la Capilla produced the 1996 bottle which was designed by Mexican artist Alejandro Gomez Oropeza, filled with Pasión Azteca tequila, and made from solid platinum and white gold.

   The newest bottle, going for $3.5 million, is made of ceramic with a 5-pound layer of platinum and more than 4,000 diamonds totaling 328 carats.

2. **Bullsh*t!** It was **never** traditional to put a worm in a bottle of tequila or mescal. The idea to put worms in bottles of mescal was drummed up by United States marketers in the 1940s. If you find a worm in your tequila, throw it away: The Mexican Standards Authority forbids the practice of putting any invertebrate life forms into bottles of tequila.

   It is true that the worm in question (actually the larval form of the *Hypopta agavis* moth, and not a worm at all but a caterpillar) feeds on the agave plant and is considered a delicacy in parts of Mexico.

3. **Fact.** Amazingly, tequila has the precise proportion of carbon, hydrogen, and oxygen atoms necessary to create diamonds.

   The scientists heat eighty-proof tequila to over 1,400 degrees Fahrenheit, which results in a very fine film of synthetic diamond. The resulting diamond crystals are far too thin to use for jewelry, but they are extremely hard and quite heat-resistant and are hoped to have a variety of industrial applications.

JELL-O!

1. When Jell-O first got its name, only four flavors were available: orange, lemon, strawberry, and raspberry. At one time or other in its history, Jell-O offered cola, celery, seasoned tomato, mixed vegetable, and Italian flavors.

2. On June 17, 1971, President Nixon declared Jell-O to be the official dessert of the United States of America in a press conference and photo op with Jell-O makers. He praised the gelatin treat for being "100 percent American."

3. Jell-O is primarily made of gelatin. Gelatin comes from the boiled bones, skins, and tendons of animals. Because gelatin is so extensively processed, the FDA does not require gelatin-based foods to be listed as animal-based.

1. **Fact.** Celery Jell-O??? Gross, but true. In the mid-twentieth century, gelatin-based salads were very popular at the American dinner table. Originally, the makers of Jell-O suggested that cooks use lime-flavored Jell-O for that purpose, but as the popularity of wriggling salads grew, the company decided to introduce savory flavors. Celery, tomato, vegetable, and Italian salad Jell-O did not last very long.

   Cola Jello-O was introduced in 1942 and lasted only a year.

2. **Bullsh*t!** There's not a shred of truth to that. June 17, 1971, is the day Nixon declared the **War on Drugs**.

   In 2001, however, Jell-O was made the official state snack of Utah.

3. **Fact.** Gelatin is hydrolyzed collagen, which is extracted from animal bones, skins, and tendons. Collagen helps to give bones, skin, and joints their elasticity, which is precisely the property that causes the food to gel together.

   Jell-O is hush-hush about where its gelatin comes from. Technically, it is possible to produce a synthetic version of gelatin, but this author is pretty sure he's enjoying cherry-flavored boiled animal tendons on a regular basis.

CHOCOLATE!

1. In 1943, the U.S. Army approached Hershey to make a chocolate bar ration for soldiers in World War II. By the end of the war, Hershey had produced over 380 million 2-ounce Tropical Chocolate Bars, which were designed to withstand temperatures of up to 120 degrees Fahrenheit without melting.

2. Chocolate is lethally poisonous to cats. We humans can enjoy chocolate to our hearts' content, but we'd better keep it far away from our pets. It can give a nasty stomachache to dogs, but it is particularly dangerous to our feline friends due to their smaller body size and the fact that a cat tongue has five times as many sweetness receptors as a dog's.

3. Chocolate comes from the seeds of the cacao tree, an evergreen tree native to tropical parts of the Americas. The cacao tree comes from the genus *Theobroma*, which means "food of the gods."

1. **Fact.** The chocolate bars remained exceptionally hard in extremely hot conditions, and were available to soldiers in the Korean War and the Vietnam conflict as well, as part of their sundries kits.

   Some veterans hasten to point out, however, that while the chocolate bar did not melt in your pocket, it did not readily melt in your mouth either, and that the taste suffered.

   The Tropical Chocolate Bar also went to the moon—on board the Apollo 15 mission in 1971.

2. **Bullsh*t!** Chocolate is **not particularly dangerous for** cats. It **is** highly toxic to them, but they are simply not interested in it. Why? **Cats cannot perceive sweetness at all.**

   Dogs are at a high risk for chocolate poisoning. A large dog would feel the effects after eating a bar of chocolate, and **could die** after eating several.

   Chocolate **is poisonous to humans**, too. You would have to consume many pounds of chocolate to feel the effects, but people still manage to poison themselves with it on a regular basis.

   The toxic culprit is the alkaloid theobromine, which is particularly present in dark chocolate and baker's chocolate.

3. **Fact.** The evergreen cacao tree (*Theobroma cacao*) is native to tropical regions of the Americas, particularly Central America.

   The tree produces large fruit pods, which are full of cocoa beans, also known as seeds.

   Theobroma comes from the Greek *theos*, meaning "god," and the Greek *bromos*, which means "food," and more specifically, "oats."

   Technically, I suppose, you could say chocolate is the "oat of the gods."

THE HOT DOG!

1. According to the American Hot Dog Society, about 2 billion hot dogs are consumed in the U.S. each year.

---

2. The name "hot dog" has its roots in the nineteenth century, when many street sausage vendors were believed to actually serve dog meat. By 1843, newspaper editors were referring to "dog-meat sausages" and "dog sandwiches."

---

3. "Hot Dog" was the name of a Saturday-morning children's documentary show starring Jonathan Winters, Jo Anne Worley, and Woody Allen. One introduction to the show included Woody Allen looking into the camera and saying, "*Hot Dog*. A program about stuff."

1. **Bullsh*t!** As far as we know, there is no American Hot Dog Society—yet. But the president of the venerated National Hot Dog & Sausage Council, Janet Riley, asserts that we eat **20 billion** hot dogs in this country each year.

   That's nearly enough hot dogs to go to the moon and back **four times**.

2. **Fact.** Whether the crafty street vendors actually served dog or not is something, I believe, best left to the shrouded mists of history. The dog-meat rumor, however, persisted throughout most of the nineteenth century.

   In the mid-1890s, it seems the slang "hot dog" was in regular use on college campuses. By 1896, both Yale and Harvard had multiple references to hot dogs in their publications, including humorous allusions to the rumor of the sausages' dubious canine provenance.

3. **Fact.** *Hot Dog* only aired for one season on NBC, from 1970 to 1971, and was later syndicated in reruns, also for one year, from 1977 to 1978.

   The pilot episode featured Allen, Worley, and Tom Smothers (of the Smothers Brothers). Winters replaced Smothers when the show was picked up. Each show was dedicated to answering kids' questions about everyday objects. Most of the music for the show was recorded by the Youngbloods.

   Hot Dog was the only TV series in which Woody Allen appeared regularly.

THE ICE CREAM SUNDAE!

1. Five American cities claim to be the birthplace of the ice cream sundae: Ithaca, New York; Evanston, Illinois; Cleveland, Ohio; Buffalo, New York; and Two Rivers, Wisconsin. In its early days the sundae was spelled multiple ways, including "sunday," "sondie," "sundi," "sundhi," and "sundaye."

2. Despite its American origin, South Koreans are huge fans of the ice cream sundae, which is a popular street food throughout the country. The Korean version is even sweeter and richer than the original.

3. New York City's Serendipity 3 restaurant features a $1,000 sundae on its menu.

1. **Fact.** Each of the five cities has evidence for its claim, but none has conclusive proof. Maybe the ice cream sundae was such a good idea that it was invented in five places at once.

   My favorite origin story is Evanston's: In the late nineteenth century, religious leaders enacted a law outlawing the sale of ice cream sodas on Sundays. (We all know what ice cream sodas can lead to.) The story goes that drug store owners started serving ice cream with syrup instead of soda, and thus obeyed the letter of the law, if not the spirit. The confection became known as the Sunday, and later the appellation "sundae," so as not to further enrage the devout.

   In the end, nobody is sure who actually invented the sundae (or why we don't still spell it "sundhi"), but I sure am glad they did!

2. **Bullsh*t!** Koreans do love *sundae* very much, and it is a popular street food in South Korea. But Korean *sundae* is nothing like the ice cream sundae. *Sundae* is made by **stuffing intestines with noodles and pig's blood**.

   Yum! Can I have hot fudge on mine?

3. **Fact.** Serendipity 3 does offer a $1,000 Golden Opulence Sundae, which is covered with edible 23-karat gold leaf, Amedei Porcelana chocolate, and rare candies. It's served in a crystal goblet, with a side of passion-fruit-infused Golden caviar.

   According to the owners, Serendipity 3 sells an average of one Golden Opulence Sundae per month.

THE APPLE!

1. Nearly every kind of apple we eat today is descended from one species, *Malus sieversii*, a wild apple that still grows in the Ili Valley of Kazakhstan. The wild apples of *Malus sieversii* are some of the largest apples available today, and the plant is especially hardy, but it is nevertheless threatened by extinction.

2. The Granny Smith apple is named after Maria Ann Smith, a nine-teenth-century farmer. She produced the apple in her Australia orchard by accident.

3. In the Book of Genesis, the serpent tempts Eve with an apple, the forbidden fruit from the Tree of Knowledge. The Norse goddess Sjöfn was said to have been poisoned by an apple and cursed to eternally roam the underworld, giving apples to the dead. The Greek god Dionysus was often associated with apples, and commonly depicted as eating or holding an apple.

1. **Fact.** *Malus sieversii* apples are big and colorful, and the tree is capable of growing and producing fruit in harsher conditions than most domestic varieties. It still grows wild in the Ili Valley in Kazakhstan (which stretches into border regions of China), but scientists and cultivators have begun to plant and study the wild apple in hopes of gaining insight into growing and breeding better apples. The apple you had for lunch is *Malus domestica*.

---

2. **Fact.** "Granny" Smith cultivated many kinds of apples, and the Granny Smith variety emerged quite accidentally as a hybrid of two different species. The apples became popular locally, winning competitions, and neighboring orchards began to acquire the seedlings and produce Granny Smiths themselves.

   Today, there are more than 7,500 cultivars of apple, of which Granny Smith is only one.

3. **Bullsh*t!** The serpent does tempt Eve with a forbidden fruit in the Book of Genesis, but nowhere is it identified as an apple. In fact, numerous religious scholars have suggested other fruits as much more likely, such as the **grape, fig, tamarind, or pomegranate**. The apple does often appear in Western artistic depictions of the story; one theory is that the choice originated as a pun, because the Latin word for apple is identical to the word for evil (*malum*).

   The Norse goddess Sjöfn was associated with love, whereas **Iðunn was the goddess of apples and youth**. Apples were associated with fertility and youthfulness.

   Dionysus, the Greek god of the harvest, wine, and ecstasy, was commonly depicted with **grapes**.

THE FORTUNE COOKIE!

1. Fortune cookies are not Chinese in origin at all. Amazingly, fortune cookies are from Japan. They stem from the tradition of *omikuji*, which are fortunes written on little slips of paper and given out at Shinto shrines and Buddhist temples.

2. In March 2005, 110 people earned the second prize in a Powerball lottery drawing, inciting panic at the Lottery Association that there was cheating going on. (Statistically, there should have only been around five second-place winners.) It turns out that nearly all the winners got the numbers they played from the same place: a fortune cookie.

3. Currently, around 800 million fortune cookies are made for export each year in China.

1. **Fact.** Fortune cookies have never been Chinese. And you won't find them there now. In fact, a recent attempt to market fortune cookies to the Chinese was met with failure. They are "too American."

Records of Japanese people making a version of the fortune cookie date back to the eighteenth century, and the practice probably began long before that.

It is still unclear precisely how the practice was adopted by Chinese restaurateurs in the U.S. One theory is that the original Japanese fortune-cookie makers in the country might have been detained during the Japanese-American internment in 1942, leaving a niche that Chinese workers filled.

---

2. **Fact.** The Multi-State Lottery Association had to distribute $19 million in unexpected payouts after winners got their numbers from fortune cookies that were manufactured by Wonton Food in Long Island City, New York. Wonton Food pumps out 4 million fortune cookies a day in their factory, and supplies them to restaurants all over the country.

When told by the *New York Times* that 110 people had won the lottery thanks to their fortune cookies, Wonton Food vice president of sales Derrick Wong said, "That's very nice!"

3. **Bullsh*t!** Fortune cookies are a distinctively American industry. The vast majority of the **3 billion made each year** are produced **here in the U.S.A.**

HONEY!

1. Honey is an ancient food. Humans have collected and eaten honey for well over 10,000 years. Honey was cultivated in ancient China and Mesoamerica, and it was a popular sweetener in ancient Egypt. The Egyptians and Assyrians sometimes used honey to embalm the dead.

2. Honey is flower nectar that has been consumed and subsequently excreted by honeybees. The nectar is consumed, pooped, consumed again, and pooped thousands of times before it adopts the viscous consistency and amber color that we like in our honey.

3. It's possible to become severely intoxicated by eating honey. Honey made from certain rhododendrons contains grayanotoxin—eating it can make you dizzy, weak, and nauseated, and cause you to sweat and vomit. Toxic honey was used (with lethal effect) as a weapon against the Roman forces of Pompey during his campaign in Asia Minor.

1. **Fact.** A cave painting in Spain, more than 10,000 years old, depicts women gathering honey. In ancient times, Mayans cultivated honeybees, which they regarded as sacred. Beekeeping was practiced in China 3,000 years ago.

   Even without refrigeration, honey in a properly sealed container can last indefinitely. In ancient Egypt and parts of the Middle East, corpses were sometimes embalmed in honey.

   It's nice to know that some mummies are sweet on the inside.

2. **Bullsh*t!** Honey is not bee poop. **Bee vomit** would be a more apt description, but still not strictly correct. **Dehydrated bee regurgitation** is pretty spot-on.

   In the hive, the nectar is regurgitated **mouth to mouth** from one bee to another, until it is deposited in the wax honeycomb.

   Thousands of bees help to dry out the nectar **by flapping their wings**. (This is why a beehive is constantly buzzing.) The result is the gloppy goo that we love so much.

3. **Fact.** In the first century B.C., the Roman legions passed through a narrow valley and came across a large cache of honey. As pillaging soldiers are wont to do, they appropriated the sweet stuff and consumed it on the spot. Little did they know the toxic honey was a gift from their enemies. As the legions fell collectively sick, they were ambushed and easily slaughtered.

   In mild cases of toxic honey, you're back to normal in twenty-four hours. In extreme cases, toxic honey can kill.

   Use "honey poisoning," on me, as an excellent and original call-in-sick excuse.

GUMMI BEARS!

1. The gummi bear was invented in 1922 by Hans Riegel in Bonn, Germany. It was originally called the Dancing Bear, which he delivered personally to customers on his bicycle. The company he founded is still around today, and is still a major international seller of gummi bears.

---

2. Gummi bears and other gummi candies contain the gelatin-friendly sweetener xylitol, which has been found to be three times as likely to cause cavities and tooth decay as regular sugar.

---

3. A North Carolina company makes and sells the World's Largest Gummi Bears. The behemoths are larger than a football, weighing in at 5 pounds and measuring 9 inches tall. One giant gummi bear has 12,600 calories, representing the equivalent of 1,400 regular-sized gummi bears.

1. **Fact.** Hans Riegel founded the Haribo company in 1920 (**Ha**ns + **Ri**egel + **Bo**nn = Haribo). Haribo gummi bears are ubiquitous and popular, and sold worldwide as Gold-Bears Gummi Candy.

2. **Bullsh*t!** The gummi bears we buy in stores do not contain xylitol, and are no more likely to cause cavities than any other candy.

   Recent scientific studies have tried out gummi bears with xylitol in them on children, and found that not only are xylitol-laced gummi bears **less likely** to cause cavities, but that the sweetener actually **fights cavities** and **prevents tooth decay**. More tests are under way.

   Soon we'll be having gummi bears before going to bed instead of brushing our teeth!

3. **Fact.** It is not known if they truly are the world's largest gummi bears, but that is the official name of the product manufactured by GGB of Raleigh. One bear has a shelf life of about a year, which is about how long you'll need to eat all ninety servings. (Or a week if you're my cousin Randy.)

THE TWINKIE!

1. In 2010, as an example for his students, a nutrition professor at Kansas State University went on a "Twinkie diet" for eight weeks, eating only junk food items from a convenience store at every meal. The result? He gained a whopping 27 pounds.

2. Former President Clinton is a fan of the Twinkie. He placed one inside his National Millennium Time Capsule, alongside the complete literary works of William Faulkner and the recordings of Louis Armstrong.

3. The urban legend that claims Twinkies have a shelf life of over ten years is patently false. A Twinkie does last longer than most baked goods, but its actual shelf life won't blow any minds: twenty-six days.

1. **Bullsh*t!** The "Twinkie diet" lasted ten weeks, and Professor Mark Haub **lost** 27 pounds. The trick? Calorie counting. By limiting himself to 1,800 calories a day, the professor reached his ideal weight, his bad cholesterol went down, and his good cholesterol went up. Haub ate Twinkies every day on the diet, as well as Nutty Bars, powdered donuts, and Doritos.

2. **Fact.** Clinton's time capsule was to be filled with artifacts, ideas, and accomplishments that represented America at the turn of the millennium. Besides Faulkner, Armstrong, and the Twinkie, future people will find a model of the Liberty Bell, the Hawaiian state flag, a picture of U.S. soldiers liberating a concentration camp, and children's artwork.

3. **Fact.** One urban legend asserts that Twinkies have a shelf life of forever, which is, of course, impossible. Twenty-six days is a long time for even a snack cake to last: Twinkies are capable of this because there are no dairy ingredients in the recipe at all.

SPAM!

1. In 2005, a limited edition flavor of Spam was issued by Hormel: Spam Golden Honey Grail. The collector's edition tin (and the sweet, sweet meat inside) was timed to coincide with the production of the Broadway musical *Monty Python's Spamalot*.

---

2. While jokesters will tell you that Spam stands for "Something Posing as Meat," the name was created in 1941 as a short form of "Supply-Pressed Ham."

---

3. Spam was a major staple during World War II for Allied soldiers. Soviet leader Nikita Khrushchev said, "Without Spam, we wouldn't have been able to feed our army." President Eisenhower said, "I ate my share of Spam, along with millions of other soldiers."

1. **Fact.** In a perfect example of "if you can't beat 'em, join 'em," Hormel got in on the fun with the coveted cans of honey-drenched mystery meat.

   Original Monty Python member and writer of the musical Eric Idle said, "Spam is the holy grail of canned meats!"

2. **Bullsh*t!** When the product was first launched, it was boringly called Hormel Spiced Ham. Hormel held a contest in 1937 to come up with a more exciting name. An actor named Kenneth Daigneau came up with Spam, **short for "Spiced Ham,"** and earned the $100 prize money.

3. **Fact.** During the war, Hormel shipped 15 million cans a week to Allied soldiers.

   Khrushchev's remark comes from his autobiography, and Eisenhower's from a 1966 letter to the then-head of Hormel, H. H. Corey. He went on to write, "I'll even confess to a few unkind remarks about it—uttered during the strain of battle, you understand. But as former Commander in Chief, I believe I can still officially forgive you your only sin: sending so much of it!"

CHAPTER 4

Famous
Dead
People

Quite a few of us consider ourselves experts on dead people, whether we conduct *séances* to communicate with them or dig up their 2,000-year-old bones to make a name for ourselves. Some clearly love dead people more than the living, including a couple of history professors I've had. (I'm talking about you, Mr. Knueven.)

To truly be an expert on dead people would be a feat indeed, since there are about 100 billion of them in all. And that's only counting the ones who've lived on *our* planet. I didn't quite have room to include everyone, so I chose a handful of the most famous people that have ever lived. I've learned quite a few little-known nuggets about the historical figures we hold dear, and also that we harbor quite a few misconceptions about them as well.

George Washington chopped down his father's cherry tree, right? Wrong. Benjamin Franklin discovered electricity? Negative. Nero fiddled while Rome burned, George Washington had wooden teeth, and Lady Godiva rode naked through the streets of Coventry?

Bullshit.

ELVIS!

1. Elvis was a black belt in karate. He picked it up during his tour of duty in Germany in the late 1950s, and later studied in Memphis under a master sensei who was a former combat trainer for Korean military intelligence.

2. Elvis recorded nearly 700 songs in his music career, but he only wrote nine of them. Interestingly, the nine he wrote were among the least popular of his recordings.

3. The FBI opened a file on Elvis Presley during his life, and eventually amassed over 600 pages on the King. There are documents in the files that denounce Elvis as a "danger to the United States."

1. **Fact.** Elvis took up martial arts under the Shotokan sensei Jürgen Seydal while fulfilling his military duties in Germany in 1958. From 1970 to 1974, Elvis trained under Master Kang Rhee in Memphis, Tennessee. Rhee once instructed Korean military intelligence officers and currently runs a dojo called Elvis Karate.

2. **Bullsh*t!** In fact, Elvis wrote **none of them at all**. In biographies and first-person accounts, he was described as lacking the patience required to craft a song from beginning to end. Instead, he preferred to take existing songs and make slight tweaks, usually to the lyrics, to help the song fit his style. Elvis is credited as a cowriter on the songs "You'll Be Gone" and "That's Someone You Don't Forget" (both B-sides), but the other writer, his bodyguard Red West, later admitted to writing the songs himself, with just the "idea" for them coming from Elvis.

3. **Fact.** The FBI does in fact have 683 pages of documents in Elvis's file. The records consist of documents relating to an attempted blackmail of the King, as well as press clippings and letters from the public to the FBI about Elvis. It is in these letters that he is identified as a "danger"; there is no evidence that the FBI itself ever investigated that particular claim.

HARRY HOUDINI!

1. Before becoming the greatest escape artist of all time, Harry Houdini was a Hungarian immigrant named Ehrich Weisz. Throughout his career, Houdini demonstrated that he could escape from any strait-jacket, pair of handcuffs, cage, or tank—often while submerged in water.

---

2. Houdini was a pioneer of aviation. He flew his own plane in 1909, just six years after the Wright brothers made history. Houdini took his plane on tour with him, and in 1910 made the first-ever pow-ered flight over Australia.

---

3. Although popular myth claims that Houdini drowned during an underwater escape attempt, he actually died of heart failure in his sleep at the age of sixty-one.

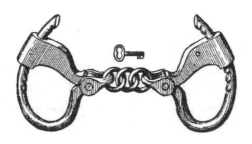

1. **Fact.** Ehrich was known to friends as "Ehry," which eventually became "Harry." He chose Houdini as a stage name out of admiration for the French magician Jean Eugène Robert-Houdin.

   While touring, Houdini would challenge local police officers to lock him in handcuffs. He always escaped. He escaped straitjackets by dislocating his shoulders and contorting his body. He was also able to swallow and regurgitate his set of lock picks.

   Now *that* takes skill.

---

2. **Fact.** Houdini took to the skies in his French biplane by 1909, not long after Orville and Wilbur Wright made the first controlled, powered flight in Kitty Hawk, North Carolina, in 1903. In March 1910, he became the first to make a controlled, powered flight over Australian soil. He famously announced he would fly from city to city on his next tour, but the plane went into storage and he never flew again.

3. **Bullsh*t!** Houdini died at the age of **52**, under somewhat **mysterious circumstances**. It is believed that he died as a result of **repeated blows to the stomach** by a college student.

   Houdini popularly claimed he could take any blow above the waist without injury. He would stave off a slug or two from very strong men simply by inhaling deeply and engaging his abdominal muscles. After a performance, a McGill University student asked him if the challenge was still on, and when he replied that it was, the student punched the unprepared magician several times in the belly. Houdini later died of complications due to peritonitis (caused by abdominal trauma) and a ruptured appendix.

HELEN KELLER!

1. Contrary to the stories about her, Helen Keller was *not* born both deaf and blind.

---

2. Despite her handicaps, Helen Keller wrote two books in her lifetime, both autobiographies: *On Your Own* and *The Secret of Inner Strength: My Story*.

---

3. Helen Keller was a Tuscumbian, a Wobbly, and a Swedenborgian.

1. **Fact.** Helen Keller was born on June 27, 1880, with both vision and hearing. She lost both at around eighteen months of age after an infection.

2. **Bullsh*t!** Helen Keller wrote at least **twelve books** during her lifetime, and numerous published letters and articles. Two of her autobiographies were ***The Story of My Life*** and ***Light in my Darkness***. *On Your Own* and *The Secret of Inner Strength: My Story* are the autobiographies of Brooke Shields and Chuck Norris, respectively.

3. **Fact.** Keller was born in Tuscumbia, Alabama, which makes her a Tuscumbian. She was a proud member of the Industrial Workers of the World union, which is also known as the Wobblies. Finally, Keller was a member of what is now known as the New Church, founded by Emanuel Swedenborg. Swedenborg was a mystic who believed he was appointed by God to create a new version of Christianity.

    Keller's book, *Light in my Darkness*, was filled with Swedenborgian philosophy.

MARIE CURIE!

1. Marie Curie was born Maria Sklodowska in Poland in November 1867. She was the first person in the world to win two Nobel Prizes. She was also the first woman to win a Nobel Prize, and the only woman ever to win a Nobel Prize in two different fields. She discovered two elements: polonium and radium.

2. The element curium, with the atomic number 54, was discovered by Marie's husband, Pierre. Curium naturally occurs in the earth's core.

3. Marie Curie's extensive work with radiation eventually led to her death. Even now, Curie's research notes, letters, and cookbooks, a hundred years old, are kept in lead-lined boxes, and any scholars who wish to handle them must wear protective clothing.

1. **Fact.** Marie Curie was the greatest female scientist ever. She won the Nobel Prize in Physics in 1903, and the Nobel Prize in Chemistry in 1911.

    Curie was a French citizen, but proud of her Polish roots. When she and her husband discovered a new element in 1898, she named it "polonium" in honor of Poland.

2. **Bullsh*t! Curium was discovered in 1944** at the University of California, Berkeley, and named after Marie and Pierre Curie. Curium's atomic number is **96**; **54** belongs to **xenon**. Curium is a **synthetic** chemical element, produced in labs for a variety of purposes. The earth's core is believed to be primarily **iron** and **nickel**.

3. **Fact.** Marie Curie pioneered the field of radiation therapy, discovering multiple beneficial effects, but did not learn quickly enough just how dangerous radiation can be. She conducted numerous experiments and handled substances for which today's scientists would need to employ a battery of safety precautions.

    She died in 1934 from either aplastic anemia or leukemia, almost certainly caused by her extensive exposure to radiation.

MICHAEL JACKSON!

1. Michael Joseph Jackson was born on August 29, 1958, to parents Joseph Walter Jackson and Katherine Esther Scruse. Jackson grew up in Gary, Indiana, and had six brothers and three sisters: Sigmund, Toriano, Jermaine, Marlon, Brandon, Steven, Maureen, La Toya, and Janet.

2. Jackson won eighteen Grammy Awards, twenty-six American Music Awards, seven MTV Video Music Awards, three People's Choice Awards, forty Billboard Awards, and three Presidential Awards; earned fourteen Guinness World Records; and was inducted twice in the Rock and Roll Hall of Fame.

3. Jackson's song "Bad" was released as a single in August of 1991. The music video was directed by Ron Howard, and the concept was inspired by the fight scenes in Shakespeare's *Romeo and Juliet*. Jackson originally intended the song to be a duet between his sister Janet and himself.

1. **Fact.** Jackson's siblings Sigmund, Toriano, Steven, and Maureen are better known as Jackie, Tito, Randy, and Rebbie, respectively. Brandon was Marlon's twin brother, and died shortly after being born.

2. **Fact.** He also won a Bambi, some Popcorns, and a few BRITs.

   Jackson and his oeuvre have earned over 375 nationally recognized major awards.

3. **Bullsh*t!** *Bad* the album was released in August 1987, and the single of the track "Bad" was released in **September 1987**. The music video was directed by **Martin Scorsese** and was inspired by *West Side Story*.

   Michael Jackson originally intended the song to be a duet between **Prince** and himself.

   I would have loved to hear that version!

THE ELEPHANT MAN!

1. "The Elephant Man" was the stage name of John W. Merrick, born in 1883 with paraneoplastic cerebellar degeneration, leaving him with a major limp and a severely deformed head. Merrick toured Europe and the United States extensively as a sideshow until his death in 1938.

2. A play about Merrick, called *The Elephant Man*, debuted on Broadway in 1979 and won the Tony Award for Best Play. In 1980, the cast took on a new member to play the part of the Elephant Man: David Bowie. A very short-lived 2002 revival starred Billy Crudup in the role.

3. A movie about Merrick, called *The Elephant Man*, premiered in 1980. It featured Anthony Hopkins and John Gielgud, was directed by David Lynch, and was produced by Mel Brooks. The movie received eight Academy Award nominations, but did not win any.

1. **Bullsh*t!** Often incorrectly remembered as "John," the Elephant Man's real name was **Joseph Carey Merrick**. He was born in **1862** and died in **1890** at the age of 27.

   Merrick's medical condition, though unknown, definitely wasn't paraneoplastic cerebellar degeneration, an autoimmune reaction that many cancer patients suffer. It has been posited that Merrick had **neurofibromatosis type 1**, **Proteus syndrome**, or both.

   Merrick spent most of his life in London, for a short time as a novelty exhibit, and he only toured Europe once—a tour that was cut short by the fact that his road manager robbed and abandoned him. He never toured the U.S.

2. **Fact.** *The Elephant Man*, by Bernard Pomerance, starred Philip Anglim, who received a Tony nomination for best actor. He was replaced by David Bowie, who made his American stage debut in the role. The production also saw Mark Hamill (Luke Skywalker from *Star Wars*) play Merrick for a time.

3. **Fact.** Merrick was played by John Hurt, Hopkins played Frederick Treves, and Gielgud played Carr Gomm, the hospital governor.

   The film was only David Lynch's second feature, but Mel Brooks reportedly loved his first, *Eraserhead*, and thought him perfect for the job. Brooks, famous for his farces and parodies, kept his name off all marketing for the film, lest people assume it was a comedy.

   The movie did not win in any of its eight Oscar categories, losing out to such films as *Ordinary People*, *Raging Bull*, *Tess*, and *Fame*.

PICASSO!

1. Though remembered as Pablo Picasso, "Pablo" was only a nickname. At birth, Picasso's full name was "Diego Ruiz Picasso."

2. Picasso joined the French Communist Party in 1944, and in 1950 he received the Lenin Peace Prize from the Soviet Union. He once stated, "I am a Communist and my painting is Communist painting."

3. While painting *Les Demoiselles d'Avignon* (*The Young Ladies of Avignon*), a 1907 oil depicting five nude prostitutes, Picasso amused himself by painting the prostitutes' faces to resemble women he knew.

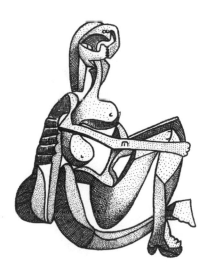

1. **Bullsh*t!** Picasso's birth certificate read "**Pablo Diego José Francisco de Paula Juan Nepomuceno María de los Remedios Cipriano de la Santísima Trinidad Ruiz y Picasso.**"

   The painter's name followed Spanish naming customs, which meant he took his mother's last name. Had he been born in the U.S., he would have had his father's last name and been known as "Pablo Ruiz."

2. **Fact.** Picasso went on to say, "But if I were a shoemaker, Royalist or Communist or anything else, I would not necessarily hammer my shoes in a special way to show my politics." According to Jean Cocteau, Picasso once said to him of the Communist Party: "I have joined a family, and like all families, it's full of shit."

3. **Fact.** The painting is now universally hailed as a masterwork, but at the time of its first public exhibition, it was deemed by many to be immoral. It is now part of the permanent collection of the Museum of Modern Art in New York City.

JIMI HENDRIX!

1. Jimi Hendrix's guitar of choice throughout his career was the Danelectro Silvertone. Most of the guitars he played were custom-made for him, left-handed and with an extra-long neck because Hendrix was so tall.

---

2. Jimi Hendrix was born Johnny Allen Hendrix on November 27, 1942. Before forming the Jimi Hendrix Experience, he played in the following bands: the Velvetones, the Rocking Kings, the King Kasuals, the Blue Flames, and the Isley Brothers.

---

3. Jimi Hendrix died on September 18, 1970. The autopsy claimed that he had consumed a large amount of sleeping pills and had asphyxiated on his own vomit. Hendrix is considered to be a part of the "27 Club," a group of legendary rock stars, all of whom died at the age of twenty-seven.

1. **Bullsh*t!** Jimi Hendrix's guitar of choice was the **Fender Stratocaster**. He was left-handed, but didn't have the luxury of custom guitars—he would usually restring right-handed guitars and turn them upside down to play!

   Jimi Hendrix was tall, but not that tall. He was **5' 11"**.

2. **Fact.** Johnny Allen Hendrix was his first name, but his father changed his name to James Marshall Hendrix when he was a toddler. As an adult, he went by "Jimmy" for a long time before changing the spelling to "Jimi."

   Hendrix played in his first band, the Velvetones, when he was a teenager. As he developed his skill, he would play in multiple bands over several years.

   Hendrix played backup guitar for the Isley Brothers in 1964, and would go on to play with Little Richard, Curtis Knight and the Squires, and Joey Dee and the Starliters before forming the Jimi Hendrix Experience.

3. **Fact.** Despite the large amount of sleeping pills, it is generally believed that his death was accidental.

   Janis Joplin, Brian Jones, Jim Morrison, and Kurt Cobain all died at age twenty-seven, and are therefore members of the "27 Club" alongside Hendrix.

WILLIAM SHAKESPEARE!

1. Shakespeare called his son "Hamlet" after the character from his play of the same name. Hamlet, who did not survive past infancy, was his only child.

2. "Advertising," "circumstantial," "compromise," "design," "employer," "engagement," "exposure," "investment," "luggage," "manager," "misquote," "negotiate," "pander," "petition," "reinforcement," "retirement," "swagger," "violation," "watchdog," and "worthless" are all words that were coined by Shakespeare.

3. The Globe Theatre, the famous place where Shakespeare's plays were produced, burned to the ground during the performance of one of Shakespeare's plays.

1. **Bullsh*t!** Shakespeare had **three children** with his wife Anne Hathaway: Susanna, Judith, and **Hamnet**, not Hamlet. The theory goes that Shakespeare named the character after his son, not the other way around.

   Hamnet died of unknown causes at the age of eleven.

2. **Fact.** In some cases, Shakespeare was literally the first person to use the word, and in others, the word had a very different meaning and he was the first to use it in the way that we use it now.

   Shakespeare also coined "addiction," "alligator," "bet," "bump," "critic," "downstairs," "embrace," "excitement," "eyeball," "generous," "gloomy," "glow," "grovel," "gust," "hint," "housekeeper," "hurry," "lonely," "obscene," "outbreak," "puke," "radiance," "scuffle," "shooting star," "tranquil," and "undress." There are many, many more.

3. **Fact.** The fire, which happened on June 29, 1613, started after a cannon was shot off during a scene in *Henry VIII*.

AL CAPONE!

1. Before he became the most notorious gangster of all time, Al Capone was a model student. He attended public school in his native New Jersey and graduated near the top of his class.

2. Al Capone died in 1947 in his Miami Beach home shortly after his forty-eighth birthday. His death was due to heart failure, which was brought on by the fact that he had pneumonia and a severe case of syphilis, and had suffered a stroke a few days earlier.

3. When Al Capone bought a house in Palm Island, Florida, the citizenry was so outraged that they hatched a plan to declare martial law and drive him out.

1. **Bullsh*t!** Al Capone grew up in **Brooklyn, New York**, and did go to public school for a time (P.S. 133), but was **expelled at the age of fourteen for hitting a female teacher**.

2. **Fact.** Capone spent part of his later life in prison (Alcatraz) after being convicted of tax evasion, but he was released early due to good behavior, work credit, and his advancing syphilis. By the time of his death, the sexually transmitted disease had damaged his brain so extensively that the FBI estimated that he had "the mentality of a twelve-year-old child."

   The stroke, the subsequent pneumonia, and the complications from his syphilis were too much for Capone to handle, and his heart gave out on January 25, 1947.

3. **Fact.** True. When Al Capone arrived in Florida in 1928, the populace was outraged. The American Legion devised a plan to declare martial law and deny Capone his constitutional rights. While he was subject to a great deal of harassment, Capone defied the local authorities and stayed right where he was in sunny Florida . . . until he took a trip to Chicago to engineer the St. Valentine's Day Massacre.

MARTIN LUTHER KING, JR.!

1. President Reagan signed Martin Luther King, Jr. Day into law in 1983, and it was first observed in 1986. Voters and lawmakers in Arizona refused to honor the holiday, which led the NFL to pull its plans to hold Super Bowl XXVII in Arizona in 1993.

---

2. Martin Luther King, Jr. was posthumously given the Nobel Peace Prize in 1969 for his message of non-violent resistance to racism, making him the first African American to earn the award.

---

3. The FBI tracked King extensively and wiretapped his telephone in the '50s and '60s in an attempt to prove he was a Communist. After his world-famous "I Have a Dream" speech in 1963, an FBI memo called King the "most dangerous and effective Negro leader in the country."

1. Fact. Martin Luther King, Jr. Day is celebrated in the U.S. on the third Monday of every month, which falls on or near his birthday, January 15.

Some conservative pundits fought hard against the holiday for a time, citing various reasons, including the idea that the holiday was just for African Americans, and that the holiday was created "illegally."

Arizona governor Evan Mecham railed against the holiday and did all he could to strike it down. At the time, Senator John McCain sided with Mecham.

The National Football League decided to move Super Bowl XXVII from the Sun Devil Stadium in Tempe, Arizona, to the Rose Bowl in Pasadena, California, after the NFL Players' Association urged them to do so, costing Arizona an estimated $350 million in major convention business.

Two years later, Arizona popularly voted to celebrate MLK Day. Super Bowl XXX was held at the Sun Devil Stadium.

2. Bullsh*t! King earned the award in **1964**, while he was very much alive, and was at the time the **youngest** person to ever receive the distinction.

The first African American to receive the Nobel Peace Prize was Ralph Bunche, who accepted it in 1950 for his work as a mediator in Palestine.

3. Fact. The FBI never managed to prove any connection between King and Communism. (He famously said, "There are as many Communists in this freedom movement as there are Eskimos in Florida.") The FBI did scoop up a lot of dirt about his private life and used it in an attempt to discredit him.

ALBERT EINSTEIN!

1. As a child, Albert Einstein was a notoriously inconsistent (and often downright bad) student, routinely receiving low grades, particularly in math.

2. In 1930, Einstein and his student Leó Szilárd patented the Einstein Refrigerator, which required no electricity and had no moving parts. Despite the breakthrough innovations involved, the Einstein Refrigerator never caught on.

3. Albert Einstein's face was a key inspiration for the facial design of both E.T. and Yoda. A photograph of Einstein's face sold at auction in 2009 for $74,324.

1. **Bullsh*t!** The persistent rumor that Einstein was a bad student is completely **false**. He did have brushes with authority a couple of times, but he was a **brilliant student with top marks** (including math). He even penned scientific papers while still a teenager, and was considered to be a wunderkind.

2. **Fact.** Einstein was dismayed to hear of a spate of accidental deaths caused by broken refrigerator seals, which could leak harmful chemicals into the home. His design with Szilárd had no moving parts, which meant no seals to break. The refrigerator did not require electricity, but, instead, a heat source (such as a gas burner).

   Unfortunately for Einstein, conventional refrigerators were becoming more and more efficient, and they remained the norm. Modern-day engineers have revived Einstein's design, however, because it is remarkably environmentally friendly. The goal is to attain greater efficiency and make them available to the developing world.

3. **Fact.** The design for the face of the iconic alien from Steven Spielberg's *E.T.: The Extra-Terrestrial* was inspired by images of Carl Sandburg, Ernest Hemingway, and Albert Einstein. The face for Yoda from *Star Wars* was initially modeled on makeup artist Stuart Freeborn's, and features from Einstein's face were eventually incorporated, most notably his eyes and eye wrinkles, in the effort to help Yoda appear wise.

   The $74,324 photograph was the iconic image of Einstein sticking out his tongue. It's the most expensive photograph of the scientist ever sold.

Fact. Fact. **Bullsh*t!**

CONFUCIUS!

1. The philosopher Confucius said, "the only things to come to a sleeping man are dreams," "even the genius asks questions," and "death is not the greatest loss."

---

2. Confucius's teachings were not widely known during his lifetime and only became popular after his death.

---

3. "Confucius," a Latinization of the philosopher's name, was first coined by Italian Jesuit priests when they translated his ideas into Latin. His actual name was Kŏng Qiū, and he was also known as Zhòng Ní.

1. **Bullsh*t!** Those quotes belong to the philosopher (and "thug life" rapper) **Tupac Shakur**.

   Quotes that **are** attributed to Confucius include: "Have no friends not equal to yourself," "The accomplished scholar is not a utensil," "The man of perfect virtue is cautious and slow in his speech," and "Without knowing the force of words, it is impossible to know men."

2. **Fact.** Although he had a few disciples at the time of his death, Confucius was an itinerant teacher, unregarded during his lifetime—and yet his philosophy ended up influencing hundreds of millions of people.

3. **Fact.** Kŏng Qiū is the real name of Confucius. Kŏng is a common Chinese family name. Zhòng Ní was his "courtesy name." There was a long-held Chinese tradition that men should be given a second name later in life as a sign of respect.

Fact. Fact. **Bullsh*t!**

RONALD REAGAN!

1. Ronald Reagan and Nancy Reagan starred in one movie together: *Hellcats of the Navy*. The prologue of the movie featured a rare appearance of Admiral Chester W. Nimitz, a five-star admiral in the U.S. Navy.

---

2. As a baby, Reagan was nicknamed "Irish" by his father because of his ruddy appearance. The nickname stuck throughout his entire youth and was resurrected during his presidency by members of his cabinet.

---

3. Reagan began his career as a liberal Democrat, and a supporter of the progressive New Deal policies. Later, he endorsed Republican presidential candidates Dwight D. Eisenhower and Richard M. Nixon while still a Democrat. He didn't become a Republican until 1962.

1. **Fact.** Ronald Reagan received top billing for the role, and Nancy Davis (as she was then known) was second-billed. The U.S. Navy worked very closely with the production team for the movie, and Nimitz's appearance in the prologue was extremely unique, since he rarely spoke publicly.

   The movie was released in 1957. The future president and Nancy Reagan had been married already for five years.

2. **Bullsh*t!** His father nicknamed him **"Dutch"** as a baby because he looked like "a fat little Dutchman." He kept the nickname throughout his childhood.

   Consequently, we can assert with conviction that no members of his cabinet ever addressed Reagan as "Irish."

3. **Fact.** When Reagan became a Republican, he stated, "I didn't leave the Democratic Party. The party left me."

   Reagan was the host of television's *G.E. True Theater* from 1954 to 1962, a role that demanded much speechmaking, most of which he wrote himself and espoused pro-business conservative ideals, such as low taxes and small government, even though he was a Democrat.

Fact. Fact. **Bullsh*t!**

CHE GUEVARA!

1. Che did not start out as a revolutionary; in fact, he intended to become a physician (and actually reached this goal before being killed at the age of thirty-nine).

2. Many people believe in the "Curse of Che Guevara" because an astonishing number of people who had a hand in Che's execution have been victims of violent accidents and, often, deaths.

3. The restaurant chain Hooters faced a bit of a scandal after launching its "Viva La Hooters" advertising campaign, which featured waitresses in Che Guevara-emblazoned bikinis. Ad executive Thomas Vail snarkily defended the campaign, saying, "We thought it was appropriate. He fought for equality; we're fighting for good times and delicious wings."

1. **Fact.** Of course, Che did more with his life than just practice medicine. He became an author, a diplomat, and, most notably, a Marxist revolutionary and guerilla warrior who fomented and/or contributed to armed conflicts in Cuba, Congo, and Bolivia. As a medical student, Che traveled throughout Latin America and the poverty he saw encouraged his radical tendencies.

---

2. **Fact.** Bolivia's president, General René Barrientos, who ordered Che's execution, died in a mysterious helicopter accident two years later. Colonel Roberto Quintanilla, an intelligence chief who fingerprinted Che, was murdered in Germany. General Juan José Torres, a member of Barrientos's joint chiefs of staff, was himself executed, as was Honorato Rojas, the farmer who revealed Che's whereabouts. General Gary Prado, who arrested Che, was shot and paralyzed from the waist down. Lieutenant Colonel Andrés Selich, who participated in Che's capture, was savagely beaten to death. Even the CIA-trained Félix Rodríguez, who helped track down and capture Che, and famously took his picture with Che's corpse, claimed that he developed asthma suddenly afterward. He had never had asthma before, while Guevara suffered from it his whole life. The man who shot Che to death, Mario Terán, to this day lives in hiding, apparently afraid of the curse.

3. **Bullsh*t!** Hooters has never, to my knowledge, launched a Che advertising campaign.

   In a bizarre twist of irony, these days you can find images of Che, who gave his life to fighting capitalism, on just about every conceivable kind of commercial product out there, **including bikinis**, as Gisele Bündchen so provocatively demonstrated during Fashion Week.

NAPOLEON!

1. Before Napoleon Bonaparte became the emperor of France, he was actually born with the name Napoleone di Buonaparte to parents Carlo Buonaparte and Letizia Ramolino on the island of Corsica, giving rise to the argument that Napoleon was actually *Italian*.

2. Napoleon spent the last few years of his life in exile on the isle of Saint Helena. There were numerous plots to rescue him, including one that hoped to spirit him away in a *submarine*. He died in 1821, before the plot could be carried out.

3. Napoleon was extremely short, even for his time. A theory that he was aggressive *because* of his height led psychiatrists to coin the phrase "Napoleon complex." Experts have posited that as much as 9 percent of the United States population suffers from the syndrome.

1. **Fact.** Corsica was traded to the French in 1764, but the island resisted. France took complete control in 1770, the year after Napoleon was born. Napoleone di Buonaparte changed his name to Napoleon Bonaparte while he was in his twenties, in order to sound more French. His parents were of noble Italian ancestry.

2. **Fact.** An American inventor, Robert Fulton, had developed one of the first versions of the submarine ever, the *Nautilus*, for Napoleon in 1800. Although the prototype was successful, the military lost interest in it.

   After Napoleon's exile, French Bonapartists commissioned a smuggler named Tom Johnstone to rebuild the *Nautilus* and use it to rescue the former emperor. Unfortunately, Napoleon died before the plan came to fruition.

3. **Bullsh*t!** The idea that Napoleon was comically short is **false**. Historians estimate that Napoleon was around 5' 6", which, at the time, was the **average** height for men. British propaganda of the era derisively portrayed Napoleon as extremely short, which is the most likely source of the ongoing misconception. Historians also note that Napoleon was often accompanied in public by his personal guard, who were elite soldiers and of above-average height, which would make him appear short by comparison.

   The "Napoleon complex" is primarily a **cultural invention**, and is not an actual syndrome recognized by psychiatry. There is no professional consensus on its existence, let alone its prevalence.

ANNE FRANK!

1. Anne Frank was born Marie Anna Frank on August 12, 1932 in Amsterdam. In 1945, the Nazis took over the city, and the Frank family went into hiding in a secret two-room attic above the house of a family friend, where they remained for sixteen months. In 1946, the hiding place was discovered by accident, and Anne Frank and her family were arrested and sent to Nazi concentration camps.

2. When the Nazis arrested the Frank family, they scattered her diary pages all over the floor of the Secret Annex. Although apparently they intended to destroy the book, they ended up making it possible for the diary to be pieced back together and published under the name *The Annex* after Anne's father was released from Auschwitz.

3. In 1958, Holocaust deniers, as part of their ongoing assertions that Anne Frank never existed, challenged Nazi-hunter Simon Wiesenthal to find the man who arrested her. Wiesenthal found the Nazi arresting officer, Karl Silberbauer, in 1963. Silberbauer recalled Frank vividly, and even reported that he had told her father, "What a lovely daughter you have."

1. **Bullsh*t!** Anne Frank was born **Annelies Marie Frank** on **June 12, 1929** in **Frankfurt, Germany**.

   The family fled to Amsterdam in 1933, after Adolph Hitler came to power in Germany.

   In **1942**, Frank and her family went in hiding in a secret **three-story, five-room apartment on top of an office**. The family was in hiding for **two years and one month**.

   Their hiding place was **betrayed by a secret informant**, and the family was arrested and sent to concentration camps. Anne Frank died of typhus at the age of fifteen while in the Bergen-Belsen concentration camp.

2. **Fact.** Miep Gies, a family friend and former employee of Anne's father Otto Frank, and one of the people who hid and protected the Franks, was able to collect the scattered diary pages. She saved them and gave them to Otto Frank when he returned to Amsterdam after the war ended. Before it would be published worldwide as *The Diary of Anne Frank*, it was published as *The Annex*, and then as *The Diary of a Young Girl*.

3. **Fact.** For years after its publication, Holocaust deniers and Nazi sympathizers openly challenged the idea that the diary was written by a young girl, and, in fact, asserted that Anne Frank never existed at all.

   Wiesenthal's discovery of Karl Silberbauer dealt a major blow to their claims. In an effort to erase all doubt, several groups applied both forensic tests and handwriting analysis to the manuscript, proving each time that the diary was real, and written by Anne Frank.

Fact. Fact. **Bullsh*t!**

WALT DISNEY!

1. Before he created Mickey Mouse, Disney had created a character named Oswald the Lucky Rabbit. Disney created several cartoons for the character before he lost the rights to the rabbit in a budget dispute with Universal. Disney started from scratch, creating Mickey, and deliberately designed him to be extremely similar in personality and appearance to Oswald.

2. Disney was a progressive visionary not just in business, but in politics. He supported workers' rights as a way to support families—because he relied on families doing well to make his fortune.

3. The last two words that Walt Disney scribbled down before he died in 1966 (from complications due to a heart attack) were "Kurt Russell." The actor Kurt Russell said, "I don't know what to make of that."

1. **Fact.** Disney had recently begun his own animation studio when he signed with Universal to make a series of cartoons starring Oswald the Lucky Rabbit. When Disney asked Universal for an increase in budget, he was coldly informed that he would be forced to take a budget *cut*, and that almost all of his animators had been secretly signed to direct contracts with Universal.

   Disney, ever proud, turned them down, and lost most of his animators along with his star character. He started over from scratch and created Mickey, who was very similar in appearance to Oswald.

   Of course, history shows that Disney had the last laugh. Mickey was an instant hit, and Oswald became only a footnote in the annals of animation.

2. **Bullsh*t!** Disney was a staunch conservative. When workers at his studio engaged in a strike, he called it an example of "Communist agitation," even taking an ad out in *Variety* to proclaim it so. In reality, his **animators were receiving lower wages than their counterparts** at other companies, and Disney had a reputation among them as a hamhanded and insensitive boss.

   Disney and his anti-Communist alliance issued a pamphlet called the "Screen Guide for Americans," with the goal of instructing filmmakers on how to avoid Communism in their films. Rules in the pamphlet included: "Don't smear wealth," "Don't glorify the collective," and "Don't deify the common man."

3. **Fact.** At the time, Kurt Russell was a child actor signed to the Disney studio. Nobody knows what Disney meant by writing down those words.

Fact. Fact. **Bullsh*t!**

MARILYN MONROE!

1. Marilyn Monroe, born Norma Jeane Mortenson, married twice: once to the baseball player Joe DiMaggio and later to the playwright Arthur Miller.

2. Monroe was found dead in her bedroom on August 5, 1962. She was thirty-six years old. Her death was ruled a suicide, and no official major inquiry was launched. However, conflicting testimonies, evidence at the scene, and the information learned from her autopsies show that Monroe was almost certainly murdered or else killed accidentally.

3. To pay the rent during her early years in Hollywood, she posed for nude photographs as Mona Monroe.

1. **Bullsh*t!** A child of foster homes, Monroe **first married at age sixteen, to James Dougherty**, in order to gain her independence. According to reports, his mother, a family friend, had asked him to marry her so that she would not have to go to an orphanage when the foster family caring for her could no longer keep her.

2. **Fact.** Here are just a few of the pieces of evidence that are suspicious:

Monroe was found dead on her stomach in bed (with her hand resting on the telephone), but the autopsy showed that she died on her back. Her housekeeper, Eunice Murray, was present when she died, and she had changed the linens on the bed after Monroe died, washing the dirty sheets before she called the police. Monroe's psychiatrist and Murray spent four hours with the body before calling police.

The autopsy concluded that the lethal amount of barbiturates in her system (enough to kill ten people) had not been swallowed, and must have entered her body a different way. Prescription bottles were littered around Monroe's nightstand, but there was no drinking glass at the crime scene and the water was off in the house. The autopsy also ruled out injection, leaving a suppository or an enema as the only possibility.

LAPD officer Jack Clemmons, who was first on the scene, stated that it was "the most obviously staged death scene I have ever seen."

Eunice Murray was evasive during questioning, changed her story many times, and then left the country immediately.

3. **Fact.** Before she landed big roles, Monroe posed nude to make ends meet.

Fact. Fact. **Bullsh*t!**

THOMAS JEFFERSON!

1. Thomas Jefferson was a governor of Virginia, the first secretary of state, the second vice president of the United States, the third president of the United States, and the principal author of the Declaration of Independence.

---

2. Jefferson was an extremely outspoken proponent of the abolition of slavery and of the integration of blacks into American society. He wrote several essays on the subject, including *An Address to the Public from the Pennsylvania Society for Promoting the Abolition of Slavery, and the Relief of Free Negroes Unlawfully Held in Bondage* as well as *A Plan for Improving the Condition of the Free Blacks*, both from 1789.

---

3. Jefferson created the Jefferson Bible by cutting massive sections out of his own Bible with a razor while he lived in the White House. Congressman Keith Ellison was sworn into office with a copy of Thomas Jefferson's personal Koran.

1. **Fact.** That one was a gimme!

2. **Bullsh*t!** All of those things can be accurately said about **Benjamin Franklin**.

   Thomas Jefferson was deeply racist and **bought and sold hundreds of slaves in his lifetime**, and **rationalized slavery** more than once. He did eventually acknowledge that slavery should be discontinued, famously saying, "We have the wolf by the ear, and we can neither hold him, nor safely let him go. Justice is in one scale, and self-preservation in the other." He argued that blacks could not live in the same society as whites, and that freed slaves should be deported and resettled in Africa.

3. **Fact.** Jefferson was famously pragmatic and intellectual in his approach to religion. In creating the Jefferson Bible, he distilled it to just the moral teachings of Jesus Christ and removed all references to mysticism, miracle, or magic, such as the virgin birth.

   Ellison, a U.S. representative from Minnesota, is the first Muslim to be elected to the federal government. He chose the Koran from Jefferson's library in hopes to counteract opposition to his use of a Koran at all. It didn't work: Virginia Representative Virgil Goode and a score of conservative pundits called it a threat to American values.

   It's not surprising that Jefferson owned a copy of the Koran—as a man of learning he would have studied any book that has such a huge influence on the world.

CLEOPATRA!

1. The most famous Cleopatra—subject of numerous movies, plays, histories, and books—was queen of Egypt during the Classical period. While never a pharaoh (pharaohs had to be men), she considered herself to be a reincarnation of the Egyptian goddess Anuket.

2. Cleopatra was married to two of her own brothers while they were young boys. Three of her four grandparents were siblings, and she only had four great-grandparents. (You and I have eight.)

3. After the deaths of Mark Antony and Cleopatra, their children were adopted by Octavia, Mark Antony's former wife, whom he had abandoned to be with Cleopatra, and who was also the sister of Octavian, the man Mark Antony and Cleopatra had gone to war against.

1. **Bullsh*t!** Cleopatra ruled Egypt during the **Hellenistic** period. She was Greek, and not only was she a pharaoh, but she was the **last pharaoh** Egypt ever had. After her reign, Egypt became a Roman province. Cleopatra often represented herself to be the reincarnation of the Egyptian goddess **Isis**.

2. **Fact.** At the time, it was common for royal families to form incestuous unions and engage in inbreeding. Doing so kept the royal bloodline "pure" and kept the balance of power more squarely in the hands of one family. Of course, then, as it would now, the practice resulted in numerous stillborn babies and birth defects.

   History shows that Cleopatra married her brothers Ptolemy XIII and Ptolemy XIV to keep with tradition only. Technically, each marriage made them co-rulers of Egypt, but she kept the power for herself.

3. **Fact.** The three children of Cleopatra and Mark Antony were indeed cared for by his former wife after the two committed suicide. Cleopatra's son by Julius Caesar was killed.

Fact. Fact. **Bullsh*t!**

MOZART!

1. Wolfgang Amadeus Mozart was born Johannes Chrysostomus Wolfgangus Theophilus Mozart in January 1756. He composed over 625 works in his lifetime, the first being "Andante in C," which he wrote when he was *five years old*.

2. Peter Shaffer's play based on Mozart's life, *Amadeus*, premiered on Broadway in 1976, and ran for a total of 490 performances. Mozart was played by Barry Bostwick, and Salieri by George C. Scott. It was nominated for four Tony Awards, but only won one: best actor for Scott.

3. Mozart was extremely bawdy with friends and family, and had a tremendous fondness for scatological humor. He composed a canon in B-flat for six voices called *Leck mich im Arsch*, and also wrote the lyrics to Wenzel Trnka's *Leck mir den Arsch fein recht schön sauber*, each of which roughly translate to "Lick Me in the Ass" and "Lick My Ass Nice and Clean," respectively.

1. **Fact.** To be fair, "Andante in C" was only ten measures long, and, though composed by Mozart, was written down by his father.

   Mozart, with more than 600 works, was extremely prolific, but Georg Philipp Telemann is said to have composed more than 3,000 works. Telemann, however, lived more than twice as long as Mozart.

2. **Bullsh*t!** Peter Shaffer's *Amadeus* premiered on Broadway in **1980** and ran for just shy of **1,200 performances**. The production starred **Tim Curry** as Mozart and **Ian McKellan** as Salieri. It was nominated for **seven** Tony Awards, and won **five**, including best actor (McKellan), best director (Peter Hall), and best play.

3. **Fact.** Mozart wrote several other bawdy songs, and frequently made scatological references in his letters, signing off on a love letter to his cousin with the following: "By the love of my skin, I s**t on your nose, so it runs down your chin."

   Many scholars and historians have been thoroughly baffled (and, likely, embarrassed) by Mozart's stinky side, seeing that he was such an elegant, refined, and accomplished member of the courts. Others have decided that it was precisely *because* of the stuffiness of polite society that he turned to such humor.

   To me, it says he was human, and for that makes him all the more likable.

AMELIA EARHART!

1. Amelia Earhart was a founder (and in 1931 was elected the first president) of the Ninety-Nines, an organization for the advancement of women pilots, which still exists to this day. Members during Earhart's time included Opal Kunz, Bobbi Trout, and Pancho Barnes.

2. Amelia Earhart created and marketed her own fashion line and a luggage collection, she was a celebrity endorser for Lucky Strike cigarettes, and she was an associate editor for *Cosmopolitan* magazine.

3. Amelia Earhart disappeared over the Indian Ocean, somewhere near Heard Island, in 1932 during an attempted transatlantic flight in a fixed-wing Du Temple Monoplane.

1. **Fact.** The organization got its name from the number of charter members, ninety-nine. Since its inception, the Ninety-Nines has had over 20,000 woman pilot members, and has 179 chapters in sixteen countries.

    The Ninety-Nines Inc. maintains and operates the Amelia Earhart Birthplace Museum.

---

2. **Fact.** Earhart was one of the first celebrities to endorse and market a fashion line. Amelia Earhart Fashions was carried at Macy's. Amelia Earhart Luggage was advertised as being "built *like* a plane—not just *for* one." She used *Cosmopolitan* as a forum to promote women in aviation.

3. **Bullsh*t!** Amelia Earhart disappeared in **1937**, over the **Pacific Ocean**, near **Howland Island** in her attempt to **circumnavigate the globe**. She was flying a Lockheed Model 10 Electra.

    Heard Island is a barren Antarctic Australian territory in the Southern Ocean.

    The Du Temple Monoplane was a steam-powered aluminum plane built in 1874—it made the first successful powered flight in history, but it was only airborne for a short while. It could never make it around the world.

    Most planes nowadays are fixed-wing. It simply means that the wings don't flap or rotate.

GANDHI!

1. Gandhi's full name was Mohandas Karamchand Gandhi. The word "mahatma" is an honorific name that comes from the Sanskrit *mahātmā*, meaning "great soul."

2. In the 1982 film *Gandhi*, the role of Gandhi was played by Krishna Pandit Bhanji, who won the Academy Award for Best Actor for his performance, beating out Dustin Hoffman, Peter O'Toole, Paul Newman, and Jack Lemmon. *Gandhi* also won the Academy Award for Best Picture that year, beating out *E.T.: The Extra-Terrestrial*.

3. In 1893, Gandhi traveled to South Africa to help combat the discrimination against the native blacks. In a series of articles, Gandhi lambasted the country's treatment of native Africans, and organized resistance to the British war against the Zulus.

1. **Fact.** Mahatmas are thought of as spiritual leaders. Recognized mahatmas are very rare, but Gandhi was not the only one. The nineteenth-century had Mahatma Jotiba Phule, a philosopher who contributed to the development of education and women's rights in India.

---

2. **Fact.** This was a trick one—bonus points go to those of you who already knew that Krishna Pandit Bhanji is the real name of actor Ben Kingsley. He adopted "Ben Kingsley" for his acting career out of fear that his ethnic-sounding name would limit the roles available to him.

3. **Bullsh*t!** Gandhi traveled to South Africa at the age of twenty-four for a job. He decided to stay, however, in order to help combat discrimination against **Indians** in the country.

   In fact, at the time, Gandhi was **racist** against blacks. Gandhi petitioned the British to **let Indians join them in their war against the Zulus**. When the British refused, Gandhi decided to personally lead an ambulance corps to give aid to the British wounded.

   It should be noted that all of this was early in Gandhi's life, and only illuminates the power of transformation: Later in life, Gandhi would speak openly in support of both native Africans and American blacks, and to vehemently condemn racism against either.

BORING!

1. Edwin G. Boring was an experimental psychologist and psychology historian who popularized the idea that different parts of the tongue are responsible for different basic tastes. His work with visual perception led to some optical illusions being called "Boring figures."

2. Wayne Boring was a native Minnesotan and a successful comic book artist, doing the pencil work for the Superman comic strip in the '40s and '50s and lending his pencil to Captain Marvel and Prince Valiant.

3. In 1994, graduating high school senior Peter Eastman was asked how he'd like his name written on his diploma. He decided to go with the obvious: "William Boring." He subsequently legally changed his name and has been William Boring ever since ("Billy" Boring to his friends). When asked why the change by an NPR interviewer, he said, "My father, his father, and his father are named Peter Eastman. And so I'm saying I'm my own person. I'm Boring."

1. **Fact.** Boring (1886–1968) was a leader in the field of experimental psychology and was a director of the Harvard psychology lab for more than twenty years.

   The popular image that can be seen as either an old lady's face or a young woman in profile is a Boring figure.

   The idea that we use different parts of our tongues to taste different things is a misconception that resulted from Boring's mistranslation of a German research paper. We taste every type of flavor from all parts of the tongue (which means my fourth grade teacher was wrong!).

---

2. **Fact.** Boring (1905–1987) was credited with having a huge effect on the visual tone of Superman, and subsequently on our perception of the hero.

3. **Bullsh*t!** The statement is mostly true, except for one crucial error. Peter Eastman did not change his name to William Boring, **he changed his name to "Trout Fishing in America."** That's Trout America for short, and Sensei Trout in Japan, where he teaches English.

   "Trout Fishing in America" is certainly not the weirdest name out there. Just ask the Swedish parents who named their baby "Brfxxccxxmnpcccclllmmnprxvclmnckssqlbb11116."

CHAPTER 5

PHYSICAL
SCIENCES

Weird

Science

It is generally agreed upon, particularly by scientists themselves, that every field of science is, in the grand scheme of things, still in its early infancy. Scientists, as a rule, search for demonstrable, provable truth about the world, but few would say we know anything with *certainty*, because all human knowledge is fallible. If there's one thing science is excellent at, it's frequently proving its own prior conclusions to be quite wrong.

That being said, people who are full of distrust and skepticism when it comes to the scientific body of knowledge in general are perhaps the most glorious examples of human stupidity in the world. For example, when I was a teenager, a letter from the Flat Earth Society arrived at our house. The society wanted our support in their mission to spread the word that scientists are crackpots and the world is, obviously, flat. Otherwise, we'd fall right off of it! And things would forever be rolling away from us, right? I thought it was a hilarious joke.

But they weren't joking, and still aren't. The Flat Earth Society is still active today. My sister is a planetary geologist, and I can tell you, from direct experience, that she is a verifiable expert that can prove to you by multiple methods that the earth is round (in fact, an oblate spheroid) and that she is not some sort of steeple-fingered trickster out to deceive us.

Real science can be amazing, unbelievable, and downright weird. Turn the page and see for yourself.

Fact. Fact. **Bullsh*t!**

THE SUN!

1. The sun is a class GV star, which is also known as a "yellow dwarf." The term is a misnomer because the sun is in fact *not* yellow, but white, and while it may be a dwarf compared to giant stars, the sun and other yellow dwarfs outshine 90 percent of the stars in our galaxy.

---

2. The sun is not only moving, it's a speed demon. It is currently traveling hundreds of miles per second through an area called the Local Bubble Zone.

---

3. Hear that ticking? The sun is actually a time bomb of a sort—it is contracting and cooling down, and will eventually undergo a gravitational collapse and explode into a supernova, which will destroy the earth. But don't panic. We have 10 billion years to prepare for our fate.

1. **Fact.** The sun is, in fact, white, and only appears yellow to us due to atmospheric scattering of blue light. Most of the stars in our galaxy are red dwarfs, which are not nearly as bright as the sun.

---

2. **Fact.** Our planet orbits the sun, and the sun orbits the center of the Milky Way. While it takes the earth roughly 365 days to orbit the sun, it takes the sun roughly 250 million years to complete its orbit. The sun is traveling at roughly 230 miles per second—fast enough to travel from New York City to L.A. in eleven seconds.

   The sun is actually traveling through the Local Interstellar Cloud, which is, in fact, in the Local Bubble Zone, which is in the Orion Arm, which is in the Milky Way, which is in the Local Group, which is in the Virgo Supercluster, which is only one of millions of superclusters in the observable universe.

3. **Bullsh*t!** The sun actually **does not have enough mass to explode as a supernova**. We do have reason to worry, however, and less time to prepare. The sun will **heat up and expand**, and in about 5 billion years it will officially become a red giant. While the earth will not be blown up, it will likely be swallowed up by this enormous version of the sun—if our planet is spared that fate, it will only have to deal with minor inconveniences: The oceans will boil away and the atmosphere will escape.

PLASTIC SURGERY!

1. When it comes to plastic surgery, "plastic" is derived from the Ancient Greek *plastikos*, which means "to shape or mold." It has never referred to the synthetic material we know as plastic. Like its Greek root, plastic surgery is surgery that is concerned with form and shape, and is not always purely cosmetic.

2. In 2007, a Colorado man, Thomas Martell, had his thumbs surgically made smaller so that the large man could more easily operate his smart phone.

3. In 2008, U.S. citizens spent nearly $12 billion on cosmetic procedures, surgical and nonsurgical. Of the cosmetic surgeries performed, breast augmentation was the most popular, with over 350,000 procedures performed in 2008. Liposuction was a close second, with over 340,000 procedures performed.

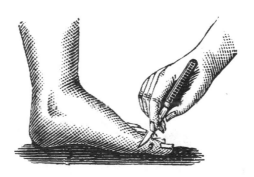

1. **Fact.** Many forms of reconstructive surgery are in fact plastic surgery, particularly when dealing with burns or disfiguring injuries.

2. **Bullsh*t!** This story was, in fact, reported in the *North Denver News* in 2007, but it was a parody. Not everyone got the joke, however, and the story circulated as truth online for a long time (and probably still does).

3. **Fact.** The data was collected by the American Society for Aesthetic Plastic Surgery, working in conjunction with a private research firm. They found that from 1997 to 2008, there was an 80 percent overall increase in cosmetic surgeries, but that there was a slight decrease in surgeries from 2007 to 2008. Racial and ethnic minorities only accounted for 20 percent of the total cosmetic procedures performed in 2008.

    The most popular cosmetic surgeries, in order, are breast augmentation, liposuction, blepharoplasty (eyelid surgery), rhinoplasty (nose job), and abdominoplasty (tummy tuck).

LIFE!

1. The oldest-known currently living individual organism is a tortoise on the Galapagos Islands named Daddy (185 years old). In close second is a giant sea urchin in the Florida Keys named Juliet (179 years old).

2. In 2010, biologist Craig Venter created the world's first synthetic life. An alarmed President Obama asked for a special commission to investigate the implications and possible dangers of the new frontier.

3. "LIFE" is the name of an interplanetary mission being developed by the Planetary Society to test the panspermia hypothesis—that life can survive being hurtled through space and can naturally transfer from one planet to another (inside of meteors or asteroids, for example). Some adherents to the idea of panspermia believe that life may have originated on the earth in this very manner, having arrived from somewhere far, far away.

1. **Bullsh*t!** While tortoises and sea urchins can live a long time, the oldest-known currently living individual organism is **Methuselah**—a **Bristlecone Pine** that will turn an estimated **4,843 years old** in 2012. Methuselah is growing in the **White Mountains of eastern California**. A Norway spruce (named Old Tjikko) has been discovered in Sweden that is estimated at **9,550 years old**—this is the oldest living *clonal* tree, in a sense a series of genetically identical trees, growing from a single root system.

2. **Fact.** Venter and his colleagues, after fifteen years and $40 million of work, created a synthetic bacteria genome out of chemicals and implanted it in the hollowed-out cell of a different kind of bacteria. The new bacteria sprang to life. As Venter put it, "This is the first self-replicating species that we have had on the planet whose parent is a computer."

   Because this process could potentially lead to biological weapons, Obama asked the Presidential Commission for the Study of Bioethical Issues to explore the dangers and implications of the discovery.

3. **Fact.** "LIFE" stands for the Living Interplanetary Flight Experiment. In the experiment, the Planetary Society will send canisters of living microorganisms on a three-year mission from the earth to the Mars moon Phobos and back.

GOLD!

1. In some cultures, people eat powdered gold, sprinkling it on fruit and other food items. The practice is harmless.

2. Gold is extremely *ductile*, which means it can be hammered into a very thin layer without breaking. Gold is so ductile that it would take less than 4 pounds of gold to stretch a wire from Los Angeles to New York City.

3. Ambergris, better known as apple glass, is an expensive golden-hued decorative material made by mixing gold with molten glass.

1. **Fact.** However, gold has no nutritional value, and it can't be digested. It just, you know, passes on through.

---

2. **Fact.** According to the American Museum of Natural History, 1 ounce of gold could be spun into gold wire 50 miles long and 5 microns thick. New York and L.A. are roughly 2,450 miles apart. It would only take 49 ounces of gold, or just slightly over 3 pounds.

   Of course, 5 microns thick means a wire so thin you wouldn't be able to see it. Maybe it's already there?

3. **Bullsh*t!** As Victorian glassblowers knew, when you mix gold (or more accurately, gold chloride) with molten glass, the result is **cranberry glass**, which is an expensive glass that is visually striking thanks to its deep, rich, **red** hue.

   Ambergris is a smelly, waxy substance produced in the digestive system and regurgitated by sperm whales. *Mmmm*, whale vomit.

CLONING!

1. Dolly the sheep, born in 1996, was the first mammal to be artificially cloned by somatic cell transfer. (Somatic cell transfer means that the cloned nucleus came from an adult and was placed in an egg cell from the same species.) Since then, many mammals have been cloned, including the first domestic cat in 2001, the first horse in 2003, the first dog in 2005, and the first camel in 2009.

2. Researchers at Kyoto University announced plans in 2011 to resurrect a species that's been extinct for 10,000 years—the wooly mammoth. Using cloning technology, they claim to be able to produce a living specimen by 2017.

3. In 2007, the House of Representatives approved the Declaration on Human Cloning, which passed through the Senate and was written into law in 2008. The federal law bans reproductive cloning, and, as far as we know, there are no (and have not been any) human clones in the United States.

1. **Fact.** Dolly made headlines in 1996, but CC the cat, Prometea the horse, Snuppy the dog, and Injaz the camel will go down in history as well as the first artificially produced clones of their kinds.

---

2. **Fact.** The researchers, led by Akira Iritani, plan to insert a preserved mammoth cell nucleus into an elephant egg cell, creating an embryo with mammoth genes. Then they'll insert the embryo into an elephant's uterus, sit back, and wait for magic.

It seems like a lot could go wrong, but Iritani is confident. "Preparations have been made," he told reporters rather ominously. "We need to discuss how to breed it and whether to display it to the public."

3. **Bullsh*t!** Actually, there are at least half a million human clones in the country right now. You probably know one or two. Biologically speaking, **identical twins are clones**, albeit naturally occurring ones, since they are descended from one zygote and share identical DNA.

The House of Representatives has tried to pass a bill banning both reproductive and therapeutic human cloning on multiple occasions, but the Senate has never let it pass. There is no federal law banning human cloning, but several state laws ban it.

Mature human embryos have been produced by artificial cloning in the U.S. **many times**, but they have never been implanted, and have never been born. The embryos are, however, human clones.

Of course, there's no telling what's going on in Area 51. They probably have human clones riding around in hovercrafts with hood-mounted laser guns.

PI!

1. Givenchy markets a cologne named Pi, calling it "the thinking man's fragrance."

---

2. In 2010, a Japanese man set a world record by calculating the value of pi to a billion decimal places. He managed this feat on his own personal laptop, which took a week to finish the job.

---

3. As of 2010, the Guinness World Record for pi memorization is held by a Chinese graduate student who successfully recited pi to 67,890 places. It took him twenty-four hours and four minutes to recite. A Ukrainian man was recognized in 2006 by the *Ukrainian Book of Records* for having memorized pi to 1 million places.

1. **Fact.** Givenchy's Pi is a "modern masculine blend of tangerine, neroli, rosemary and tarragon." Smells like smarts to me!

2. **Bullsh*t!** Japanese system engineer Shigeru Kondo and U.S. computer science student Andrew Yee set a world record by calculating pi to **5 trillion** decimal places. Kondo built a powerful computer specifically for the task that cost $18,000 in parts, including twenty external hard disks. The process took more than ninety days. No currently-available laptop could accomplish such a feat by itself.

3. **Fact.** Lu Chao had planned to recite over 91,000 digits, but made an error on the 67,891st digit.

   Andriy Slyusarchuk, a Ukrainian neurosurgeon, was not content at 1 million. In 2009, he claimed to have pi memorized to 30 million places. Although recitation is not possible, he reportedly was able to recite any random selection of the digits asked of him. He was rewarded by a visit and a meeting with Ukrainian president Viktor Yuschenko.

PEE!

1. From the seventeenth to the nineteenth centuries, stale human urine was a common household product. The aged pee, called lant, had multiple uses, including cleaning floors, rinsing hair, as an additive to ale, and as an ingredient in the making of pastries.

2. Pee has less bacteria and fewer microorganisms than the water coming out of your kitchen faucet.

3. Human urine is high in acetic acid, which has the peculiar quality of neutralizing the sting of a jellyfish. A jellyfish encounter with the skin leaves behind tiny stingers, which can keep firing long after the jellyfish is gone. Acetic acid causes the stingers to shut down. For this reason, urinating on a jellyfish sting is the best thing one can do for pain relief.

1. **Fact.** Lant has a high ammonia content, making it great for cleaning. It was often used as a hair rinse and you can still find urea listed on many shampoo bottles. Today the urea is synthetic, though.

Apparently, some hardcore pub-crawlers of the time loved the flavor of pee in their brew—ale could be single- or double-lanted, according to taste.

Lant was used in pastry recipes to help the glaze stick. Yum!

---

2. **Fact.** Urine is sterile when it comes out of your kidneys. It only becomes contaminated after contact with bacteria on your skin—or if you have an infection of some sort.

3. **Bullsh*t!** It's an old wives' tale. Some people have reported relief from peeing on a jellyfish sting and many others have not. According to scientists, urinating on a sting can actually make the pain **worse**.

Urine does not contain acetic acid—that's the primary ingredient of **vinegar**, which is also touted as a remedy for jellyfish stings. Jellyfish stings do leave behind tiny stingers, called **nematocysts**, which can continue to inject venom after the jellyfish is gone. Acetic acid (in vinegar, not pee) can neutralize the nematocysts in some jellyfish stings, but can make things worse in others.

Any change in the balance of solutes (i.e., saltiness) can cause nematocysts to sting. For this reason, rinsing the sting with fresh water is **not** recommended. Urine is largely fresh water.

If you get stung by a jellyfish, have some dignity and don't piss yourself.

P!

1. P is the symbol for the chemical element phosphorus, which has the atomic number 15. Phosphorus can be distilled from urine.

---

2. p is the symbol for momentum in physics. Momentum is the product of the mass and velocity of an object. Therefore: $p = mv$.

---

3. P is the symbol for the Paratore constant, which is the magnitude of electric charge per mole of electrons. It is handy in the study of electrolysis.

1. Fact. Yes, P can be distilled from pee. Urine is high in phosphates. Phosphorus is a basic element and can be found on the periodic table of the elements, indicated by P and its atomic number, 15.

---

2. Fact. This is true in classical mechanics, but gets much more complicated in relativistic mechanics, where you have to account for the Lorentz factor (γ).

The formula in relativistic mechanics is $p = \gamma m_0 v$.

If you disagreed with the statement based on that criteria, then you are too smart for this book and should go back to grading papers now.

3. Bullsh*t! The statement is true about the **Faraday constant**, which has the symbol **F**. F is also what you get if you guessed this statement was true.

ELECTROCUTION!

1. When the metal band Crowstone played a 2008 outdoor concert in Harvey Park near Columbus, lightning struck the stage. Guitarists Greg Rahm and Mike Leach were both electrocuted instantly, and bassist John Peters knocked unconscious. Drummer Travis Kline was completely unscathed.

2. In the late nineteenth century, Thomas Edison presided over the electrocution deaths of numerous innocent stray dogs and cats, as well as a few cattle and horses. He concluded the gruesome demonstrations with the 1903 public electrocution of a Coney Island elephant named Topsy.

3. When murderer Pedro Medina was executed in 1997, the electric chair, Old Sparky, malfunctioned. Witnesses reported that foot-high flames shot from Medina's head.

1. **Bullsh*t!** The event is fictional. Greg Rahm, Mike Leach, John Peters, and Travis Kline are all members of the metal band **Struck by Lightning**.

   Crowstone and Harvey Park don't exist (as far as I know!).

2. **Fact.** Edison was himself a proponent of DC current, as opposed to Nikola Tesla's AC current. He fried all the animals in question with AC current in hopes of convincing the public that it was too dangerous for household use. His efforts (and many animal lives) were in vain, and AC current became the standard shortly thereafter.

3. **Fact.** The case went on to prove a strong argument for the continued shift away from electric chairs and towards lethal injection for executions. But Florida attorney general Bob Butterworth found the sudden PR gratifying. "People who wish to commit murder, they better not do it in the state of Florida, because we may have a problem with our electric chair," he said.

Fact. Fact. **Bullsh*t!**

THE ROBOT!

1. "Death by robot" may sound like a science-fiction idea, but it happens. In 1979, a Ford assembly line worker was knocked on the head and killed by a robot. In 1981, a Japanese factory worker was shoved into a grinder by a robot and died. And in 2008, an Australian man was shot and killed in his driveway by a robot.

2. The Defense Department is sponsoring the development of a flesh-eating robot. The robot, playfully called the "CAR-nivore," will find its own fuel sources from biomass on the battlefield, which will include corpses.

3. The word "robot" was introduced to the world in Karel Čapek's 1921 play *R.U.R.*, which opens in an artificial-human factory. The word is derived from the word *robota*, which roughly means "serf labor" and "work" in many Slavic languages.

1. **Fact.** Robert Williams's 1979 death is the first recorded death by robot. A robotic arm collided with him while it was trying to fetch a part.

   Kenji Urada's 1981 death occurred when he failed to adequately power down a robot he was working on. The robot's hydraulic arm shoved him into a grinding machine.

   In 2008, Francis Tovey built a suicide robot with instructions he found on the Internet and programmed it to shoot him. His science project was successful.

2. **Bullsh*t!** The Defense Advanced Research Projects Agency (DARPA) has sponsored the development of a biomass-consuming battlefield robot. But the robot's developers have promised that it will be strictly **vegetarian**.

   The robot is called **EATR**, which is short for "Energetically Autonomous Tactical Robot."

   The inventor of the biomass engine used in EATR (in other words, its digestive system) is Cyclone Technologies, whose CEO, Harry Schoell, had this to say: "We completely understand the public's concern about futuristic robots feeding on the human population, but that is not our mission."

3. **Fact.** Czech playwright Čapek originally wanted to call the robots *laboři*, but his brother suggested the term *roboti*. *R.U.R.* stood for *Rossum's Universal Robots*, but the creatures in the play would be better described today as androids.

DENTISTRY!

1. Working in Pakistan in 2006, researchers from the University of Poitiers discovered what are believed to be dental tools along with skulls, demonstrating evidence of sophisticated tooth extraction dating to 500 B.C., and indicating that dentistry was practiced more than 2,500 years ago.

2. The first dental school in the world was the Baltimore College of Dental Surgery, founded in 1840. The institution was the first to issue a Doctor of Dental Surgery degree (DDS) and is still in operation as part of the University of Maryland.

3. Contrary to popular assumption, our teeth are not made of bone. They are made up of four major components: enamel, dentin, cementum, and pulp. But no bone at all.

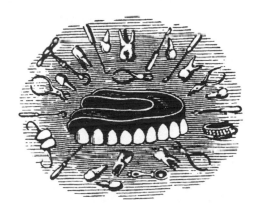

1. **Bullsh*t!** The University of Poitiers team found out that dentistry is **much older than 2,500 years**. They discovered eleven molars from a Neolithic graveyard in Pakistan with perfectly drilled holes, dating to **7000** B.C., indicating that sophisticated dentistry occurred more than **9,000 years ago**.

   The prehistoric dentists used flint-tipped drills connected to rods and bowstrings to make holes that modern dentists have dubbed "amazing" in their quality. Anthropologists believe that the skill of the work might be due to the expert bead-working skills that prehistoric people of the area possessed. Smoothing of the teeth show that the patients (or should we say "victims"?) continued to chew for a long time after their visit to the "dentist."

   Too bad that modern anesthesia would not be invented until the nineteenth century.

2. **Fact.** BCDS was, in 1840, the first school in the world to offer a science-based education in dentistry. Dentistry was practiced long before that, which makes me wonder: Who taught those dentists?

   The second school was Philadelphia Dental College, founded in 1863, and now a part of Temple University and called the Kornberg School of Dentistry.

3. **Fact.** The visible part of our teeth is the enamel, which is the hardest substance in the human body. Underneath it is the dentin, a calcified tissue that is actually yellow in color. Cementum is a calcified substance that forms around the roots of our teeth. Finally, pulp is at the center of our teeth and is made up of living connective tissue and cells.

BACTERIA!

1. The bacteria *Escherichia coli*, commonly called *E. coli*, was discovered in 1933 by Antonie van Leeuwenhoek and named after the Dutch artist M.C. Escher. It is one of the most virulent strains of bacteria known. Being infected by even a tiny amount of *E. coli* will likely lead to major sickness including fever and diarrhea, and it carries life-threatening risks.

2. Anthrax, syphilis, cholera, leprosy, the clap, Rocky Mountain spotted fever, and the bubonic plague are all caused by bacteria.

3. There are approximately five nonillion (5,000,000,000,000,000, 000,000,000,000,000) bacteria on the planet. There are more bacteria cells on or in your body than there are any other kind of cells making up your body.

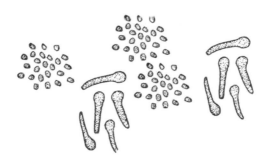

1. **Bullsh*t!** *Escherichia coli* was discovered by a pediatrician named **Theodor Escherich in 1885**, and was eventually named after him. Antonie van Leeuwenhoek was a seventeenth-century scientist who was the first to observe any kind of bacteria.

   Only certain strains of *E. coli* lead to food poisoning or sickness. In fact, ***E. coli* exists harmlessly in the intestinal tract of most warm-blooded animals**. Humans are typically colonized by *E. coli* within forty hours of birth, and the bacteria stick around until we die.

   So gaze down at your navel and wave hi to the little guys!

2. **Fact.** Those diseases and conditions, ranging from annoying to awful, are caused by the bacteria *Bacillus anthracis*, *Treponema pallidum*, *Vibrio cholerae*, *Mycobacterium leprae*, *Neisseria gonorrhoeae*, *Rickettsia rickettsii*, and *Yersinia pestis*, respectively.

3. **Fact.** The number of bacteria on the planet was estimated by the report "Prokaryotes: The Unseen Majority." The five nonillion bacteria represent a huge portion of the world's biomass.

   Scientists estimate that we have as many as ten times the number of bacteria as human cells in our body.

   In truth, we're just giant collections of bacteria walking around.

FINGERNAILS!

1. The record for the world's longest nails on a single hand belongs to Evgeny Kolyadintsev of Moscow, whose nails were over 6 feet long on his right hand.

---

2. Fingernails grow between three and four times faster than toenails. The nail on your index finger grows faster than the one on your pinkie.

---

3. Fingernails and hair are made of the same substance, keratin.

1. **Bullsh*t!** The record for the world's longest nails on a single hand belongs to Shridhar Chillal of India, whose nails were **over 20 feet long** on his left hand (his hand became disfigured from carrying around the weight, and he got out the nail trimmers in 2000). The record for the world's longest nails on both hands belongs to Lee Redmond, of Salt Lake City, Utah, whose nails were, **on average, 30 inches long**. When she was involved in a car accident in 2009, she survived, but her freakishly long nails didn't.

2. **Fact.** The speed of nail growth directly corresponds to the length of the actual finger or toe. The longer the bone, the faster the nail grows.

3. **Fact.** Fingernails and hair are both made up of a protein called keratin. It's also the main ingredient in the outer layer of your skin. Keratin comes in both soft and hard varieties, which is why your hair can be so soft and bouncy and your nails can be as tough as . . . well, nails. Certain fungi eat keratin, which is why it can be hard to get rid of athlete's foot.

Fact. Fact. **Bullsh*t!**

LASERS!

1. The term "laser" began as an acronym. L.A.S.E.R. stood for "Light Amplification by Stimulated Emission of Radiation." Less well known, but equally important, is the maser, the name of which also comes from an acronym ("Microwave Amplification by Stimulated Emission of Radiation"). The maser emits coherent microwave radiation, while the laser emits coherent visible or infrared light radiation.

2. Researchers at Harvard have managed to control the actions of worms without wires or electrodes, using nothing but laser light. The system they designed is known as the "CoLBeRT" ("Controlling Locomotion and Behavior in Real-Time") after TV personality Stephen Colbert.

3. Although laser weapons are common in science fiction, at our current level of technological advancement, any kind of actual laser weapon is impossible. Lasers can be used to enhance weapons (laser scope) or even to trigger them, but laser light itself cannot hurt or kill.

1. **Fact.** The maser was actually invented first. When the laser was invented, the term "optical maser" was suggested, but "laser" was adopted instead.

---

2. **Fact.** The researchers at Harvard's Center for Brain Science genetically modified the neurons of nematode worms, favoring worms with an inherent gene that produces light-sensitive ion channel proteins. The worms are "programmed" to respond to different wavelengths of light with different actions (such as turning left, stopping, etc.).

   So if you see a Harvard scientist pointing a laser at you, run away. (Unless, of course, that's exactly what he wants you to do.)

3. **Bullsh*t!** Even a laser pointer can hurt (particularly if it hits your retina).

   The air force initiated the YAL-1 airborne laser system in 1996. The YAl-1 is a giant laser mounted on a Boeing 747, designed to destroy airborne tactical ballistic missiles. In January 2010, the system successfully destroyed two test missiles.

   The ZEUS laser was the first laser weapon deployed by the military, and was used with great success in the Iraq War, although primarily to heat up and detonate land mines.

   The Mobile Tactical High-Energy Laser, or MTHEL, is under development by the U.S. military and Israel, and has the purpose of shooting down missiles and aircraft.

   Handheld laser guns are not around yet because of the extraordinary power they would need to operate. Laser beams themselves can heat and cut (I should know, I had LASIK eye surgery).

   In 1995, the United Nations issued the Protocol on Blinding Laser Weapons, with the express purpose of banning the use of lasers to blind enemies.

HICCUPS!

1. Forget holding your breath or drinking a glass of water upside down. Medical studies have unveiled an unlikely but effective treatment for uncontrollable hiccups: digital rectal massage.

2. Iowa farmer Charles Osborne had the hiccups during waking hours for sixty-eight years. Until his death in 1991, it's estimated he hiccupped 500 million times.

3. The word "hiccup" comes from the Latin *hic*, which means "breath."

1. **Fact.** Yes, "digital" as in fingers, and "rectal" as in butt. There are a handful of cases in which a "rectal massage" has shown to cure hiccups.

It seems this discovery was a happy accident. A sixty-year-old man was admitted to the hospital with acute pancreatitis and immediately fitted with a nasogastric tube. Hiccups commenced, and continued for two days. Multiple treatments were attempted (including a spoonful of sugar), to no avail. Finally, during a routine rectal examination, the hiccups abruptly stopped. A few hours later, they began again. The rectal exam was repeated, and the hiccups again stopped.

A report on the subject from the Bnai Zion Medical Center in Haifa, Israel, called "Termination of Intractable Hiccups with Digital Rectal Massage," outlines the details of this new and exciting remedy. The doctors in the report "suggest that this maneuver should be considered in cases of intractable hiccups before proceeding with pharmacological agents."

---

2. **Fact.** Despite traveling to doctors all over the country to look for a solution, Osborne never encountered a permanent solution to his hiccups, which began in his late twenties. He hiccupped about twenty times a minute, on average, for nearly seven decades. The hiccups subsided each night as he slept, only to return in the morning.

3. **Bullsh*t!** The word "hiccup," first alternately spelled "hiccough," is actually an onomatopoeia from the seventeenth century. (An onomatopoeia is a word that, accidentally or on purpose, sounds like its meaning.) Invented to describe the sound of a hiccup, the word has no relation to previous words or languages.

Hic is the Latin word for **"here."**

VIAGRA!
(also known as sildenafil)

1. Viagra's not just for bedroom performance: Professional athletes use the drug to enhance their athletic ability, and the little blue pills are under investigation as to whether they should be considered performance-enhancing, and therefore be banned.

2. Sildenafil was first developed at Pfizer as a treatment for hypertension and angina. During its clinical trials, researchers noticed that the drug was ineffective for treating those conditions, but that it was producing penile erections. Subsequently, they decided to market it for erectile dysfunction.

3. Sildenafil is a crystalline tropane alkaloid which inhibits phyllosilicate hydroxyl ($Al_2Si_2O_5(OH)_4$), a protein which regulates blood flow to the penis. Besides Viagra, sildenafil has been marketed under the brand names Levitra, Vivanza, and Cialis.

1. **Fact.** According to the *New York Daily News*, anonymous sources report both Roger Clemens and Barry Bonds used the drug to enhance on-field performance, and Italian cyclist Andrea Moletta was accused of "doping" with Viagra.

   Major League Baseball and the Giro d'Italia do not specifically ban Viagra, but the World Anti-Doping Agency is investigating the idea that the drug would enhance athletic ability.

   Some Viagra experts assert that the drug would have very little benefit to athletes and that any benefit would be a case of the placebo effect.

2. **Fact.** The drug was patented in 1996 and approved by the FDA as a treatment for erectile dysfunction in 1998. It was the first-ever oral treatment for ED.

   Although not particularly effective as a treatment for regular hypertension and angina, the drug has been approved as a treatment for pulmonary hypertension, and is marketed for that purpose under the name Revatio.

3. **Bullsh*t!** Viagra is **not** a crystalline tropane alkaloid, but a much more dangerous drug, **cocaine**, is. It's not a phyllosilicate, which is a mineral, and it is not $(Al_2Si_2O_5(OH)_4)$, that's the chemical representation of **dickite**. Sildenafil is a selective inhibitor of cyclic guanosine monophosphate (cGMP)-specific phosphodiesterase type 5 (PDE5), an enzyme that regulates blood flow to the penis. Sildenafil is marketed as Viagra, but Levitra and Vivanza are brand names for vardenafil, and Cialis is a brand name for tadalafil.

THE MILKY WAY!

1. The official name is the Milky Way Galaxy, which is actually redundant in a way: The word "galaxy" comes from the post-classical Latin *galaxias*, which means "milky way." The Greek root *gala* means "milk."

2. The Milky Way is the galaxy we live in, and at its center is a supermassive black hole named Sagittarius A*. The entire galaxy is 100,000 light years in diameter, and our sun is just one of the estimated 200–400 billion stars in it.

3. English is the only language in which we refer to the galaxy as the "Milky Way." In other languages it is known as the "Diamond Finger," the "Thousand Layers of Paper," the "Iron Shirt," the "Deity's Palm," and the "Nephrite Belt."

1. Fact. The ancients dubbed our galaxy the Milky Way because of the visible milky patches of night sky, which were actually millions of stars. A Greek version of milk was *galaktos*, which should sound familiar if you are *galaktos*-intolerant.

---

2. Fact. Sagittarius A* (pronounced A-Star) has the asterisk because there is technically no way to *prove* that the black hole is there, although most space experts believe it is. (If you called this one the lie based on that criteria, you're probably wearing a lab coat and should stop procrastinating and get back to your experiments now. Besides, Stephen Hawking thinks it's there, and that's good enough for me.) Sagittarius A* is only about 26,000 light years from the earth.

One hundred thousand light years is incredibly wide. It's 587,862,537,318,360,800 miles! It's shaped like a disk, too. Depending on what you're measuring, it's only between 2,000 and 12,000 light years across.

If you think an estimation of between 200 and 400 billion stars is pretty broad, you're right. We still have plenty to learn about our home!

3. Bullsh*t! All of those are moves or skills in **Shaolin Kung Fu**.

Many other languages call our galaxy the Milky Way, but there are a lot of creative names as well, that derive from ancient legends: In Cherokee, it is *Gi`li´-utsûñ´stänûñ´yï*, or "Where the Dog Ran." In Hungarian, it is *Hadak Útja*, or the "Way of the Warriors."

MIND CONTROL!

1. In 1999, a team at the University of California, Berkeley, led by Yang Dan managed to control the mind of a cat with a complex series of electrodes directly connected to the cat's brain. The team was able to make Bella sit, stand, walk, and turn both left and right with commands entered into a keyboard.

2. A team at the Freie Universität Berlin has produced a car that you can drive with your mind. The program is called BrainDriver.

3. As brain-computer interface technology gets cheaper and cheaper, several toy companies have jumped in the mix with mind-control games, including Mattel's Mindflex and the Star Wars Force Trainer from Uncle Milton Industries.

1. **Bullsh*t!** That would be cruel.

   Yang Dan's team at UCB did do something awesome with cats, however: They decoded "messages" from firing neurons in cats' brains and were able to **produce images and movies** of **what the cats see**.

   Holy crap, that's awesome.

2. **Fact.** The team, led by Raul Rojas, tricked out a Volkswagen Passat with some serious technological bling. The primary equipment is the driver's headset, which is wirelessly connected to a computer interface. The headset measures electromagnetic signals from the brain, which, after calibration, mean different things to the software. Hence, the driver can think "slow down" or "turn left" and watch the car comply.

   The Passat is also outfitted with video cameras, radars, and laser sensors that help the car "know" its surroundings and help the driver with adjustments, such as the severity of a turn, for example.

   Unfortunately, the mind-controlled car is not street-ready: There is a short delay between the thought and the car's execution of that thought (not something you want on the highway), and it's still not possible to apply a lot of detail to your instructions to the car.

   Still, I want one.

3. **Fact.** Both toys use electroencephalography (EEG) technology to read your brain waves. With an EEG headset, you can control the speed of a fan, which blows a Styrofoam ball into the air, giving the illusion of telekinesis.

   The Star Wars Force Trainer comes with the added delight of hearing Yoda's voice praise your performance.

PREGNANCY!

1. On May 14, 1939, Lina Medina of Peru gave birth via caesarean section to a healthy 6-pound baby boy. There would have been nothing exceptional about the pregnancy if not for the fact that Ms. Medina was five years old at the time.

2. In 1988, in the tiny African nation of Lesotho, a fifteen-year-old girl gave birth to a healthy boy via caesarean section. There would have been nothing exceptional about the pregnancy if not for the fact the girl had no vagina, and subsequently no apparent way to become pregnant.

3. In 2008, in India, Omkari Panwar gave birth to twins, a boy and a girl, via caesarean section, and there would have been nothing exceptional about the pregnancy if not for the fact that Ms. Panwar was eighty-one years old at the time.

1. **Fact.** Medina remains the record-holder for the youngest mother ever to give birth. The birth was well-documented, and prominent physicians from around the world traveled to examine her and confirm that the five-year-old had indeed given birth.

Lina Medina's parents raised her and her son as sister and brother.

---

2. **Fact.** The girl suffered from a congenital malformation called Müllerian agenesis, which led to her having only a dimple where her vagina should be. In other words, there was no access to her reproductive organs between her legs.

She had visited the hospital **nine months earlier** to be treated for stab wounds to the abdomen. She reported that she had performed oral sex on her boyfriend immediately prior to being stabbed by her ex. This led doctors to conclude that **sperm had traveled from a wound in her belly to her reproductive organs**.

While skeptics may doubt the possibility of such an unlikely pregnancy, a girl with no vagina became pregnant, and the skeptics have not offered an alternate theory as to just how it happened.

3. **Bullsh*t!** Panwar was not eighty-one: That would be ridiculous. We can still be amazed, though, because **she was seventy years old** at the time. In a strange coincidence, Rajo Devi Lohan, also of India, gave birth to a healthy daughter in 2008 as well, and Lohan was **also seventy years old**.

FLAMETHROWERS!

1. Concerned about the potential for disastrous floods as a result of heavy snowfall, the mayor of Boston, James Curley, sent a letter to the president of M.I.T. (Massachusetts Institute of Technology), asking him to assign a group of engineers to the task of melting snow drifts. The mayor's suggestion? Flamethrowers.

2. Detroit inventor Charl Fourie unveiled a hood-mounted flamethrower for cars (maintaining that it was intended for self-defense only), and received thousands of orders, but was prevented from making them due to a federal law making personal possession of flamethrowers illegal.

3. The modern flamethrower was invented in the early twentieth century, but massive tubed flamethrowers were used as early as 424 B.C., and the Byzantine navy had sophisticated brass-tubed flamethrowers mounted on their ships by 672 A.D.

1. **Fact.** In 1948, the new year brought massive snowfall with it, and Mayor Curley was apparently desperate. I can't think of anything that might go wrong by unleashing flamethrowers on the Boston streets, can you?

   His idea was perhaps not that far-fetched. Today you can buy the BareBlaster Ice Torch and scorch the heck out of your driveway, if you want.

2. **Bullsh*t!** Fourie **did** invent a vehicle flamethrower, called the Blaster, in 1998, in his native **South Africa**. The Blaster was not hood-mounted, but spewed flame from underneath the side-doors (for the purpose of deterring carjackers).

   His first customer was a police superintendent, and he received a lot of media attention, but in the end only sold a few hundred units before moving on to his next invention: a pocket-sized personal flamethrower.

   By the way, in the U.S., there is **no** federal law against private individuals owning flamethrowers.

3. **Fact.** Ancient Greek historian Thucydides wrote about a massive siege engine built by the Boeotians, in which a bellows propelled burning resin and pitch up the length of a hollowed-out beam of wood, spouting fire on enemy fortifications. This was used to devastating effect against the Athenians in the Battle of Delium in 424 B.C.

   The Byzantine naval flamethrowers were dominant and effective, winning for them multiple sea battles during the Byzantine-Arab Wars.

   The modern flamethrower was invented by German scientist Richard Fielder in 1901.

THE ATOM!

1. The atom is made up of subatomic particles called electrons, protons, and neutrons. Electrons are the lightweights of the bunch: It takes over 1,800 of them to equal the mass of one proton.

---

2. An atom is so small that it would take roughly a quadrillion (1,000,000,000,000,000) hydrogen atoms to tip the scales at 1 pound. A human hair is about 10 million carbon atoms thick. An estimated 2×10^{30} atoms make up the Earth.

---

3. Nuclear fission is a nuclear reaction during which the nucleus of an atom splits apart. Fission can cause an exponentially growing nuclear chain reaction, something the world has experienced firsthand in the form of the atomic bomb.

1. **Fact.** Protons and neutrons have about the same mass, and they significantly outweigh electrons. If an electron had the mass of a small jelly bean, a proton would weigh the same as that 2-liter bottle of Diet Coke in your fridge!

2. **Bullsh*t!** Too heavy, too narrow, and too few. It would take nearly **300 septillion** (300,000,000,000,000,000,000,000,000) hydrogen atoms to weigh a pound.

   A human hair is only about **1 million** carbon atoms thick. A sheet of thin aluminum foil is less than 200,000 aluminum atoms thick.

   Written out, 2×10^{30} would be a 2 with 30 zeroes after it (2,000,000,000,000,000,000,000,000,000,000), or 2 nonillion. In truth, Jefferson Labs estimates that the earth has **1.33×10^{50}** atoms, or **133 quindecillion**, which looks like this:

   133,000,000,000,000,000,000,000,000,000,000,000,000, 000,000,000,000.

3. **Fact.** When the nucleus of an atom is split (fission) the fragments travel away from one another extremely rapidly. In an atomic bomb, neutrons freed by the split collide with other nuclei, causing them to split in a successive exponential chain reaction. The motion of all the fragments traveling so quickly apart from one another is converted to X-ray heat, which is what makes the bomb so destructive.

Fact. Fact. **Bullsh*t!**

MAGNETS!

1. When magnets were first discovered in ancient Greece, they were lodestones, which were naturally occurring magnetized minerals. Lodestones were prized for their "magical" properties and were used to make the first magnetic compasses.

2. While the very first credit cards were magnetic, these days the "magnetic strip" on the back of your credit card is not actually magnetic at all. The strip is made of injection-molded plastic, which stores information in a series of tiny bumps and valleys.

3. In a groundbreaking 2010 study, neuroscientists at the Massachusetts Institute of Technology discovered that magnets can alter your sense of morality. When participants' brains were subjected to strong magnetic fields, they were more likely to judge a morally dubious scenario as acceptable, and vice versa.

1. **Fact.** Lodestones are made of magnetite, which is partly iron. These lodestones were found in Magnesia, so they were called *Magnes lithos*, for "Magnesian stone." Over the years, the word simplified to "magnet" and entered our language that way.

2. **Bullsh*t!** Injection-molded plastic with information stored in miniscule bumps and valleys is the mechanism at work with **audio CDs**.

   The first credit cards were **not magnetic** at all—they were like business cards with a person's account information written on it, allowing him to use credit at a specific store.

   Today, the strip on the back of your credit card is, in fact, made up of **thousands of tiny magnets**, encased in plastic. The technology is quite similar to the magnetic tape in an audio cassette or VHS movie.

   Just like when a tape deck spools the tape through to "read" the music, you are playing your credit card for the point-of-sale reader when you swipe it at the grocery store.

3. **Fact.** The scientists used the magnetic fields to target the part of the brain that has been linked to moral judgment.

   When volunteers were subjected to the magnetic fields, they had a harder time separating intentions and outcomes in hypothetical scenarios. For example, when told that a woman tried to poison her friend, but the friend wasn't harmed, magnetized brains were more likely to judge the situation as morally acceptable.

   I think this proves why Magneto is such a dastardly villain.

BLOOD!

1. One of the primary functions of our blood is to carry oxygen from the lungs to the parts of the body that need it. When our blood is carrying oxygen, it is bright red. When it is not, our blood is a much darker red, with slight traces of blue. In general, our blood is never totally blue. Our veins that appear blue are not actually blue—it's an optical illusion.

---

2. A biotech company called Arteriocyte has come up with a way to produce synthetic blood by "farming" it from umbilical cords. If FDA-approved, the process could eliminate the need for donating blood in the near future.

---

3. There are about 8 gallons of blood in the human body. It would take 68 million mosquito bites to completely drain the average human of blood.

1. **Fact.** Our blood is red because of hemoglobin, an iron-rich protein in our red blood cells. The presence of oxygen makes those cells an even brighter red.

   It's a myth that deoxygenated blood is true blue; it is maroon, albeit sometimes with a bluish tinge.

   Some veins appear blue because of the complex way our skin absorbs and reflects light. Amazingly, they are not actually blue. If you weren't looking at them through your skin, you'd see them for what they are.

   Blood, by the way, is 55 percent plasma, which on its own is yellow.

---

2. **Fact.** Arteriocyte's technology takes hematopoietic cells from umbilical cords and puts them in a bone-marrow-like environment, with all the nutrients needed to become blood cells. In three days, 20 units of transfusion-ready blood can be produced by 1 unit of umbilical cord blood.

   The discovery was financed by—who else—the Defense Department. Mass-produced synthetic blood could be much more easily delivered to battlefields than donated blood, which needs to travel farther and can expire before it arrives. After a traumatic injury, blood loss is the cause of 40 percent of military casualties in the first twenty-four hours.

3. **Bullsh*t!** We only have **between 1 and 2 gallons** of blood in our body. It would take a mere **1,100,000 mosquitoes** to empty our bodies.

URANUS!

1. In our solar system, Uranus is the third-largest planet volume-wise, and the fourth-largest mass-wise. Uranus is the coldest of the planets, and if you lived near one of the poles on Uranus, you would have forty-two years of sunlight followed by forty-two years of darkness.

---

2. Uranus has thirteen known moons; the largest are named after characters from Homer's *Odyssey*: Odysseus, Penelope, Poseidon, Athena, and Calypso. All five major moons are made of solid rock.

---

3. Uranus has been visited only once, by a spacecraft called *Voyager 2*. It visited the Uranian system in 1986, and there are currently no missions under development for spacecraft to visit Uranus again. *Voyager 2* was launched in 1977 and still communicates with Earth.

1. **Fact.** Jupiter and Saturn take up much more space than Uranus. Neptune takes up less space, but has more mass, because it is denser. Uranus has the peculiar property of rotating on a drastically different axis than the other planets in our system. Because of this extremely sideways axis, one pole will spend forty-two years in the sun (half of the time it takes the planet to orbit the sun) and forty-two years in darkness.

2. **Bullsh*t!** Uranus has **twenty-seven** known moons (and counting), and five major ones, which are called **Titania**, **Oberon**, **Ariel**, **Umbriel**, and **Miranda**, characters from Shakespeare and Alexander Pope.

   All five moons are made of rock and **ice**, and Miranda is predominantly made of ice.

   The rest of Uranus's moons take their names from Pope and Shakespeare as well, including Ophelia, Juliet, Desdemona, Portia, and Prospero.

   Odysseus, besides being the hero of the *Odyssey*, is a crater on Saturn's moon Tethys, and Penelope is as well. Poseidon is an asteroid, and was once the name of a moon of Jupiter. Athene (not Athena) is an asteroid, and Calypso is a moon of Saturn.

3. **Fact.** In its first twelve years of operation, *Voyager 2* visited Jupiter, Saturn, Uranus, and Neptune, taking the first and most detailed pictures of each. There is still active communication between NASA and *Voyager 2*, even though it is more than 8 billion miles away.

   Scientists recently proposed a mission that would drop a "shallow probe" into Uranus. Seriously.

Fact. Fact. **Bullsh*t!**

CHAPTER 6

Sports and Other Wastes of Time

You know the stereotype: sports fans as grunting knuckle-draggers swilling beer and yawping animatedly at a television screen. They can recite every conceivable career statistic concerning some second-string quarterback who retired five years ago. And the athletes! Steroid-soaked jocks subjecting themselves and each other to trauma and torture, just for our bloody amusement. What does it all mean? What contribution does it make to society? Why do we devote so much time and passion towards childish *games*?

Is it possible that sports are more than they seem? Is it possible that the fans are *not* mindless fat-necked apes, but actually share a deeply felt, intelligent understanding of something greater than themselves?

Can you look at a figure skater and tell her she's not an artist? How about a practitioner of yoga or tai chi? Pelé in his prime used all the grace and expression of a dancer in his virtuosity.

It's true that most sports serve no starkly utilitarian purpose. But neither does the opera. And both can take us outside ourselves, beyond our everyday existence, and tell us stories, show us beauty, and encourage us to dream.

The next time you pass a sports bar that overflows with cheers and cries, think that it is perhaps full of *aesthetes* who, like the ancient Greeks, make little distinction between sport and art and are actively engaged in elevating the human race to its true potential.

Or maybe they're just beer-soaked morons.

Fact. Fact. **Bullsh*t!**

THE FOOTBALL!

1. The football is commonly referred to as a *pigskin* because similar games were played in medieval Europe, using an inflated pig's bladder as the ball. Pig bladders were used for the inside of rugby balls as late as the nineteenth century. Modern American footballs were never made out of the actual *skin* of a pig.

---

2. While few things are as iconic to America as a football, official NFL game balls are actually made in China. The process is automated: Making modern-day footballs by hand would be too difficult and dangerous for human workers. American-made footballs have not appeared in a Super Bowl since 1941!

---

3. In the NFL, no fewer than thirty-six footballs must be provided for each outdoor game. They are inspected and pressure-tested by referees two hours before the game. A minimum of twelve footballs exclusively for kicking must also be provided, shipped in a special tamper-proof box from the manufacturer that can only be opened by a referee.

1. Fact. The medieval sport was often referred to as "foot ball," and also called "mob ball," which was appropriate, because it seems that there were few rules.

A rubber bladder for the inside of rugby balls and footballs was developed in the mid-1800s because people were getting infected by diseased pig's bladders when they inflated them *by mouth*. Modern footballs are typically made of cow leather or rubber.

2. Bullsh*t! In fact, NFL game balls are still made by hand in a small Wilson factory in Ada, Ohio. Every game ball **since** 1941 has been made there. The factory produces around 4,000 footballs per day, 365 days a year.

3. Fact. Thirty-six footballs are required for outdoor games, and twenty-four for indoor. They are each tested with a pressure gauge two hours before the game.

When it comes to the twelve kicking footballs, the NFL goes so far as to stipulate that each ball must be marked with a K, and the case containing them can only be opened in the officials' locker room. This is to combat the fact that kickers were roughing up their game balls, making them softer, slightly larger, and easier to kick.

JOUSTING!

1. In a joust, competitors race their horses in a straight line toward each other, using their lances to unseat each other. A fence between them, called a *tilt*, keeps them from running into each other and is the origin of the phrase "tilting at windmills" (meaning to joust or fight for an imaginary or ridiculous reason).

2. In 2004, a jousting accident at the Texas Renaissance Festival left competitor Trevor MacDermid with a fractured skull, brain swelling, and an *inability to speak English*. Even after four surgeries and years of therapy, the Brit still can't understand or speak his mother tongue, but is able to communicate by *speaking French*.

3. In recent years, bicycle jousting has emerged as a popular underground sport, with regular competitions in New York City and other major cities. Competitors compete on asphalt or pavement with spears made of metal or PVC pipe, and often on customized, extra-tall bikes. Injuries are common.

1. **Fact.** True, all true. In Cervantes's famous novel, *Don Quixote*, the titular hero imagines the arms of a windmill to be those of a giant, and he decides to attack the monstrous creature. His somewhat saner sidekick, Sancho, tries to dissuade him.

2. **Bullsh*t!** That's either the briefest short story I've ever written or a brand new urban legend that we can spread for fun! Take your pick.

3. **Fact.** Brooklyn's Black Label Bike Club is generally considered to be the originators of the "sport," staging jousting competitions at its annual "Bike Kill" events. Some compete on mutant "tall bikes" that put them more than 8 feet in the air. That's a long way to fall.

   Other fun-for-the-whole-family competitions at underground events like "Bike Kill" are bicycle-tossing, chugging a six-pack of beer while riding, and, my favorite, the Whiplash: Each end of one rope is tied around the waist of two bicyclists who subsequently pedal away from each other as fast as they can. You can imagine the result.

Fact. Fact. **Bullsh*t!**

THE NBA!

1. Perhaps the most significant year for the NBA was 1979. During that year, the NBA adopted the three-pointer, and rookies Larry Bird and Magic Johnson joined the organization. These three factors reversed the major decline in popularity that the sport and the league were suffering.

---

2. At the time this book went to press, the record for most points ever scored by a single player in an NBA game is 100, held by legendary player Wilt Chamberlain; the record for most total points ever scored in an NBA game is 370, in a game between the Nuggets and the Pistons.

---

3. The National Basketball Association was created in 1936, and by the 1953–1954 basketball season it had a whopping twenty-six franchises based in cities large and small. Of the twenty-six from that year, only one is still operational today: the New York Knickerbockers.

1. **Fact.** The three-point field goal was adopted from the American Basketball Association, a former rival of the NBA. Earvin "Magic" Johnson was selected first overall in the 1979 draft by the Lakers. Larry Bird was actually drafted in 1978 (sixth overall) by the Boston Celtics, but waited a year before he signed in order to play his last year of college at Indiana State.

   Bird and Johnson's rivalry, and the added excitement from the three-point game, shook the NBA out of the slump it had been in during most of the '70s, when it was plagued by low attendance and poor ratings.

2. **Fact.** Wilt Chamberlain of the Philadelphia Warriors scored 100 points in his team's 169–147 win against the Knicks on March 2, 1962. That 316-point game was also an NBA record until the Detroit Pistons' 186–184 win over the Denver Nuggets on December 13, 1983. The game went into triple overtime.

3. **Bullsh*t!** In the 1953–1954 NBA season, there were only **eight** franchises, **all** of which are operational today: the Celtics, Knicks, Hawks, Lakers, Nationals/76ers, Pistons, Royals/Kings, and Warriors.

   The Basketball Association of America was founded in 1946, and it merged with the smaller National Basketball League in 1949 to create the NBA. The new league began with seventeen franchises from cities large and small, and then went through a consolidation process until it had only eight, the smallest number there would ever be.

VOLLEYBALL!

1. Volleyball was invented in 1895 by a YMCA physical education instructor in Holyoke, Massachusetts. The original name for the sport was "mintonette."

2. Volleyball was not included in the Olympics until the 1936 Berlin Games. The U.S. team easily took the gold, and the United States vs. Germany game was famously attended by Adolf Hitler himself.

3. Since 1971, the White Thorn Lodge in western Pennsylvania has hosted a wildly popular volleyball tournament annually. Over ninety teams typically participate, including high-quality players from around the world, such as Division 1 players, national team members, and European pros. One thing sets the tournament apart from all the others, however: The White Thorn Lodge is nudist, and all the participants play naked.

1. **Fact.** William G. Morgan invented the game for his classes of businessmen who were looking for an indoor sport less rough than basketball but still requiring rigorous activity. (Basketball had been invented only four years before at another YMCA in Springfield, only 10 miles away!)

   It isn't confirmed why Morgan called it "mintonette." An observer at an 1896 game noted the amount of volleying going on, and the sport was renamed "volley ball," which has since been fused into the one word we use today.

2. **Bullsh*t!** Volleyball's official debut was in the 1964 Olympics in Tokyo. The gold went to the USSR.

   Volleyball was part of a demonstration of American sports in the 1924 Summer Olympics in Paris, but there were no formal competitions.

   Hitler was in attendance at the 1936 Berlin games, but there was no volleyball played. According to reports, he was thoroughly annoyed by the success of non-Aryan athletes, particularly African-American track-and-field star Jesse Owens, who claimed four gold medals.

3. **Fact.** It's called the Nude Volleyball Superbowl, and it's held at White Thorn every year during the first weekend after Labor Day. More than 1,500 players and naked volleyball fans show up.

LUGE!

1. Luge was invented in the 1870s by a Swiss entrepreneur named Caspar Badrutt, who was looking for activities to entice travelers to his hotel in the winter.

2. Luge has been an Olympic sport since 1964. Germany has almost totally dominated the event since the beginning, winning seventy medals in the thirty-six total competitions. The United States has only won four medals in luge competition: two silvers and two bronzes.

3. Luge events in the 2010 Winter Olympics were held at the Whistler Sliding Centre in British Columbia. Competitors complained that the forty-year-old track was too slow, and recorded some of the worst times in the history of luge competition.

1. **Fact.** Badrutt's hotel in St. Moritz, Switzerland, became one of the first winter resorts; before Badrutt's influence, it was not a normal practice to spend the winter someplace cold. The story goes that guests began using delivery sleds (items would be dragged through the snow on the sleds) for their own recreational use, which resulted in numerous collisions and accidents with people on the mountain. Badrutt organized rules and events around the idea of sledding, and the luge was born.

   Badrutt's resort also paved the way for modern-day recreational skiing.

---

2. **Fact.** It's hard to say what makes Germans so incredible at sliding around on their backs. Maybe it's something in the water. Austria's in second place, with eighteen medals. Several countries participate that have never medaled, including France, Japan, and Switzerland.

3. **Bullsh*t!** The track was relatively **newly built** (first run in 2007) and produced the **fastest luge speeds** ever recorded. The highest speed belonged to Manuel Pfister of Austria, **154 kilometers per hour**, which is about **96 miles per hour**.

   The track was so fast that it led to a fatality: Georgian luger Nodar Kumaritashvili flew off the track during a training run and collided with a steel pole. Despite its dangerous profile, deaths during luge are relatively rare. Kumaritashvili's death was the first since 1975.

ARCHERY!

1. In archery, a certain kind of target is called a "butt," which is where the expression "butt of the joke" comes from.

---

2. When shooting at a target with a traditional bow, you do not want to aim directly at the bull's-eye. In order to strike the center, you need to aim the arrow a little to one side.

---

3. The technical term for a fan of archery is "arctophile."

1. **Fact.** Reassure yourself with the knowledge that, when you're the butt of a joke, you're merely a target and not an ass.

---

2. **Fact.** This phenomenon is known as the Archer's Paradox. A right-handed archer should aim to the left of the target, and vice-versa.

   Even though an arrow feels rigid, it flexes quite a bit when it is loosed. The bowstring moves just a little bit sideways when the archer's fingers let go, which causes the arrow to flex accordingly. This is good, since it helps the arrow stay clear of the bow itself when it takes off. After that first flex, the arrow will flex the other way, turning it back on course. The arrow in flight continuously oscillates, flexing slightly less each time, until it finds its mark.

3. **Bullsh*t!** An arctophile is someone who loves **teddy bears**.

   An archery buff is a **toxophilite**. The term was coined in the 16th century and comes from the Greek *toxon* for "bow" and *philos* for "loving."

THE YO-YO!

1. The yo-yo as a toy is extremely old. The National Archaeological Museum of Athens in Greece has a terra cotta yo-yo that is dated to 500 B.C. There are drawings of yo-yos in ancient Egyptian temples.

---

2. The following are all legitimate yo-yo tricks: the Spirit Bomb, the Gerbil, the Kurukuru Milk, Dr. Tidal Wave, the Kwijibo, and the Iron Whip.

---

3. The yo-yo was used as a weapon for a long time. In the sixteenth century, hunters in the Philippines would sit in tree branches and strike their prey with a yo-yo. The word "yo-yo" actually comes from the Chinese *yuht yúh*, however, meaning "back back."

1. **Fact.** The yo-yo goes way back! There's no telling who created the first yo-yo, but it is believed to have originated in China. Yo-yos were popular in Europe by the late eighteenth century, and the first yo-yos were produced in the U.S. in 1866.

2. **Fact.** Though they may sound like superhero names or professional wrestling moves, all are official tricks according to the National Yo-Yo League.

3. **Bullsh*t!** It's a popular myth that the yo-yo was used as a weapon in the Philippines, but it's just not true. Filipino hunters in the sixteenth century would tie a **rope to a rock**, sit in a tree, and throw the rock at their prey. If they missed, they'd use the rope to haul the rock up again. The process calls to mind the yo-yo, sure, but a rock and a rope do not a yo-yo make.

   The word "yo-yo" is **Filipino in origin**. It is believed that the word comes from a Tagalog word meaning "return." (*Yuht yúh* is a language in Chinese, and has no relation to "yo-yo.")

THE FRISBEE!

1. The term "Frisbee" comes from a nineteenth-century baking company called the Frisbie Pie Company, founded by William Russell Frisbie. The word "Frisbee" is now a trademark of the WHAM-O company; when it originally acquired the rights to a flying disc it was called the Pluto Platter.

2. The first woman inducted into the World Frisbee Hall of Fame was Ashley Whippet, the California stuntwoman who is credited for initiating a major Frisbee craze after she performed various incredible Frisbee catches and throws at a 1974 Dodgers game. Her acrobatic skills were featured in a critically acclaimed full-length documentary called *Flying Free*.

3. Guts is a game in which two teams throw a Frisbee at each other, often with extreme velocity, in the hopes that the opposing team will fail to catch it. The sport is governed by the USGPA, or the United States Guts Players Association. Guts champions are crowned each year at the International Frisbee Tournament.

1. Fact. The Frisbie Pie Company was based out of Bridgeport, Connecticut. The company's pie tins (with the word "Frisbie" on them) were popular toys among local schoolboys.

The idea to sell flying discs as toys came from Walter Frederick Morrison. His first design was called the Whirlo-Way, and his later design was called the Pluto Platter, the rights to which he sold to WHAM-O. WHAM-O rechristened it the Frisbee.

Ultimate Pluto Platter, anyone?

2. Bullsh*t! Ashley Whippet *is* credited with helping to popularize Frisbee sports, and Ashley *did* perform amazing disk-catching stunts at Dodgers stadium, but Ashley was not a stuntwoman: **He** was a **dog**.

On August 5, 1974, Ashley and his owner, Alex Stein, hopped the fence during a Dodgers-Reds game and immediately began performing stunts in which Ashley caught the disc in a spectacular fashion. Alex was arrested, but their fame was established.

Stein would go on to create the Frisbee Dog World Championship, which continues to this day. Ashley Whippet was the champion for the first three years.

Ashley's skills were featured in an Academy Award–nominated **short** film called ***Floating Free***.

3. Fact. The sport was developed in the 1960s and continues to gain popularity. The annual tournament routinely features teams from Japan.

A non-competitive version of the sport is known as Flutterguts.

LUCHA LIBRE!

1. Colorful masked characters engaging in mock battle has been a tradition in Mexico since the days of the Aztecs, and modern professional wrestling both in the United States and Mexico spawned from the long-venerated practice of Lucha Libre. Colorful *luchador* wrestling masks in the style seen today made their first appearance in the early nineteenth century.

2. The most famous Lucha Libre fighter of all time was Rodolfo Guzmán Huerta, with the stage name El Santo (The Saint). True to the Lucha Libre mystique, Huerta always appeared in public wearing his silver mask, only revealing his face once, at the end of his career. Huerta appeared in more than fifty Lucha Libre movies, including the (translated) titles *Santo vs. the Evil Brain*, *Santo vs. the Vampire Women*, and *Santo in the Hotel of Death*.

3. Lucha Libre wrestlers are generally divided into two types: *rudos* and *técnicos*. The *rudos* are the "bad guys" and *técnicos* are the "good guys." The three lightest weight classes are *mosca*, *gallo*, and *pluma*.

1. **Bullsh*t!** It is true that masks were a part of Aztec culture, but Lucha Libre masks did **not** evolve from Aztec masks. The sport is not ancient, and is an offshoot of professional wrestling, not the other way around. **The first Lucha Libre masks were inspired by masked United States professional wrestlers.**

   The first major Mexican professional wrestling organization, Empresa Mexicana de la Lucha Libre, was founded in 1933, and the sport gained true popularity with the advent of television in the 1950s. The mask phenomenon began when a masked United States wrestler, the Cyclone, fought in the EMLL. Fans loved the mystique, and the tradition was quickly adopted.

2. **Fact.** Huerta wrestled for nearly five decades and became an enormous celebrity and cultural icon in Mexico, spawning an animated series, comic books, and many movies. He fought his last match just weeks before his sixty-fifth birthday. Huerta was buried wearing his silver mask.

---

3. **Fact.** As a general rule, the *rudos* (rude ones) will "break the rules" and employ a brawling style, while the *técnicos* (technicians) stick to the rules, play the part of the good guy, and display much more technical proficiency.

   Mosca, *gallo*, and *pluma* mean fly, rooster, and feather, respectively and directly correspond to the terms flyweight, bantamweight, and featherweight in combat sports.

NASCAR!

1. In 2003, Danica Patrick became the first woman to compete for the Winston Cup.

---

2. NASCAR is the most popular spectator sport in the United States, and it is the second-most popular televised sport. NASCAR is regularly broadcast in over 150 countries.

---

3. Since 1965, there have been twelve driver fatalities at Daytona International Speedway, the most recent being the 2001 death of racing legend Dale Earnhardt in the last lap of the Daytona 500. There have been more than forty driver fatalities in the history of NASCAR.

1. **Bullsh*t!** Janet Guthrie was actually the first woman to race for the Winston Cup—in 1976. She finished a very respectable fifteenth.

2. **Fact.** NASCAR holds seventeen of the twenty most-attended sporting events in the country. It benefits from huge stadiums—as many as 170,000 fans can attend a NASCAR event, whereas NFL stadiums hold between 61,000 and 92,000 spectators. NASCAR is second in television viewership, behind the NFL.

---

3. **Fact.** The figures are actually surprisingly low when the inherent danger of the sport and the frequency of accidents are considered.

Still, Earnhardt's death led to a wave of new safety measures in NASCAR, the most prominent being the requirement of all drivers to wear HANS (head and neck support) devices, which help prevent whiplash of the driver's head upon impact. Earnhardt (and several other NASCAR drivers) died from a basilar skull fracture, of which the HANS device is supposed to reduce the likelihood. A second safety measure was the installation of SAFER barriers on NASCAR tracks.

SAFER stands for "steel and foam energy reduction," and SAFER barriers absorb impacts much better than concrete walls.

CLUSTER BALLOONING!

1. In July 1982, in San Pedro, California, Larry Walters attached forty-five helium-filled weather balloons to his lawn chair, cut the cord, and flew to an altitude of 3 miles. The Vietnam veteran brought sandwiches, beer, and a BB gun along with him, and eventually fired the gun at a few balloons, sending him back down to earth. He was immediately arrested.

---

2. In July 2008, in Bend, Oregon, Kent Couch attached more than 150 giant party balloons to a lawn chair, cut the cord, and flew more than 235 miles. The gas station owner brought two GPS devices, boiled eggs, and a BB gun along with him, and used the gun to shoot balloons and control his altitude, and he finally descended in the farming town of Cambridge, Idaho.

---

3. In August 2008, in Rocha, Uruguay, Adelir Antonio de Carli attached 3,000 party balloons to a chair, cut the cord, and flew more than 100 miles. The talk show host brought a bottle of wine and a wine glass with him, and landed safely in Brazil to great fanfare.

1. **Fact.** Walters was arrested and charged with numerous violations by the FAA, because his chair drifted into controlled airspace and put him directly in the landing corridor of the Los Angeles airport.

Walters became a legend, often referred to as "Lawn Chair Larry," and was interviewed by both Johnny Carson and David Letterman.

After his popularity waned, Walters ran out of money, and he eventually committed suicide in 1993.

---

2. **Fact.** It was Couch's third flight, all of which were inspired by Larry Walters. In the first flight, his descent was too rapid, and he had to parachute to the ground. In the second, he flew 193 miles but landed just short of the Idaho border, which was his goal.

3. **Bullsh*t!** In **April** 2008, in **Paranaguá, Brazil**, Adelir Antonio de Carli attached **1,000** party balloons to a chair, cut the cord, and flew **55 miles** and reached an altitude of more than 3½ miles before he lost contact with people on the ground. The **priest did not bring any wine** but brought enough food and water for five days.

Father de Carli took jungle survival and rock climbing classes to prepare him for the trip, and brought along a cell phone, a satellite phone, and a GPS device, but it was all for naught: He disappeared over the ocean.

In July of 2008, his waist and legs were discovered floating in the water by a passing oil rig. DNA tests showed that they did indeed belong to de Carli.

THE BASEBALL GLOVE!

1. While playing for the Chicago White Stockings, Hall of Fame pitcher Albert Goodwill Spalding became the first baseball star to wear a padded glove on his catching hand. Spalding had an ulterior motive: He manufactured gloves on the side and began to sell them like hotcakes. Today, his company, Spalding, is still a major sporting goods brand.

---

2. In the early days of American baseball, it was downright unheard-of to wear a glove. When players tried out the first gloves (non-padded, fingerless affairs), they were ridiculed, jeered, and called sissies. Even catchers played barehanded, and nearly all catches in a game were two-handed.

---

3. A Wake Forest study on the minor leagues showed that catcher's gloves are extremely effective at protecting the hand. Players in this position have about the same rate of hand injuries as other baseball players, despite the fact that they catch more often.

1. **Fact.** Albert Goodwill Spalding was a pitcher for the Chicago Excelsiors, the Boston Red Stockings, and finally the Chicago White Stockings. While playing for the White Stockings in 1877, he opened a sporting goods store and began to manufacture baseballs and baseball gloves. He started to use a glove in games in order to promote them.

   Today, Spalding is headquartered in Springfield, Massachusetts, makes supplies for a variety of sports, and is probably best known for its basketballs.

2. **Fact.** A catcher named George Ellard immortalized the anti-glove sentiment in his 1880 poem:
   > *"We used no mattress on our hands,*
   > *No cage upon our face;*
   > *We stood right up and caught the ball*
   > *With courage and with grace."*

   It was a stigma that was slow to disappear, but players, dealing with excruciating bruising, eventually prevailed over the mindset.

3. **Bullsh*t!** The study showed that **seven of nine** baseball catchers experience serious hypertrophy of the index finger (usually two ring-sizes bigger), and that the phenomenon only affected catchers.

   Forty-four percent of catchers had weakened catching hands due to trauma (compared to 17 percent of outfielders), and **all of the catchers** showed symptoms of nerve damage and abnormal blood flow.

ICE SKATING!

1. Ice skates were invented in 1831 by Finnish daredevil Renny Harlin. However, Finns have a long history of skating across the ice—2,000 years ago, they propelled themselves with sticks while standing on platter-shaped sleds called *valheita*.

2. Figure skating emerged as a popular sport in the second half of the nineteenth century, and the first international championship competition was held in 1896. At first, it was considered a men's sport only, and it was called "figure" skating because competitors had to draw perfect figures on the ice with their skates.

3. In 2009, a bear viciously attacked two men in Kyrgyzstan, killing one and severely injuring the other, before being shot dead by police. The bear was wearing ice skates at the time.

1. **Bullsh*t!** Ice skates **were** invented by Finns, but it happened more than **5,000 years ago**. In southern Finland, there are more lakes per unit of land area than anywhere else in the world, and the ancient Finns discovered that it was a lot more efficient to skate across a frozen lake than to walk around it. The first skates were simply animal bones tied to the feet. The Vikings became big adopters of the practice.

   Renny Harlin is the Finnish movie director who gave us *Cliffhanger* and *Die Hard*. *Valheita* is Finnish for "lies."

2. **Fact.** Figures weren't removed from competition until the '90s.

---

3. **Fact.** The bear was one of many famous Russian circus bears that have been trained to ice skate and even play hockey. The bear might have decided he was sick of skating, however, when he attacked and killed the circus director. One of the bear's trainers was critically injured when he heroically (if not intelligently) tried to intervene.

Fact. Fact. **Bullsh*t!**

TUG OF WAR!

1. The first black athlete to ever compete in the modern Olympics was Haitian-born Constantin Henriquez de Zubiera, who competed for France in the 1900 games. De Zubiera helped France earn a silver medal in a very unique sport: tug of war.

2. During a massive tug of war in Taiwan in 1997, the rope snapped and completely severed the left arms of two separate men, Yang Chiung-ming and Chen Ming-kuo.

3. Despite the fact that tug of war is popular internationally, there is no international governing body for the sport. Previous attempts to create one have failed, thanks to disagreement over the sport's rules. The most notable is TOWEL (the Tug of War Earth League), which was begun by comedian and tug of war aficionado Scott Thompson (a.k.a. Carrot Top). TOWEL has never caught on.

1. **Fact.** De Zubiera played in the games as part of the French rugby team, but decided to participate in tug of war as well.

   Tug of war, you may protest, is not an Olympic sport. But it's a little-known fact that from 1900 to 1920 it was.

---

2. **Fact.** There were an estimated 1,600 participants in the tug of war, which was part of the Retrocession Day celebration in Taipei.

   When the contest began, an estimated 175,000 pounds of force was applied to the rope, which immediately snapped. It's believed that Yang and Chen lost their arms when the rope rebounded with astonishing force. Both left arms were severed below the shoulder.

   Amazingly, after hours of surgery, both men had the arms successfully reattached.

3. **Bullsh*t!** There **is** an international governing body for tug of war, which is called the **Tug of War International Federation (TWIF)**. Over fifty countries are members of the TWIF, from Australia to Zambia and Iran to Ukraine. Tug of war could bring the whole world together in peace, if you ask me.

   I don't know if Carrot Top is a fan of tug of war or not. I do think TOWEL would be a good name for a league, though.

SYNCHRONIZED SWIMMING!

1. In modern times, the first organized synchronized swimming was called water ballet, and was as likely to be performed in lakes, rivers, and decorative water tanks as in a swimming pool. In the first official competitions, only men were allowed to compete.

---

2. In Olympic competition, the women's synchronized swimming is scored based on grace, agility, and precise timing, whereas the men's synchronized swimming is scored based on power, agility, and precise timing.

---

3. Synchronized swimming has an unlikely honorary founding father: Benjamin Franklin. Franklin was a proponent of physical fitness and an avid swimmer who sometimes performed feats and stunts in the water to impress onlookers.

1. **Fact.** It's funny to think that a sport that is now so thoroughly dominated by women was, in a way, invented by men. The first official competition in Berlin in 1891 featured only men. But many credit a particular woman for truly popularizing the sport in the modern age.

   Australian-born Annette Kellerman had the perfect background to be the mother of modern synchronized swimming: She had been both a competitive distance swimmer and a ballet dancer. In 1907, she performed in a giant water tank in New York's Hippodrome, and was an instant sensation. Afterward, interest in organized water ballet spread extremely quickly.

   Dancing in the water is likely as old a practice as dancing in general. There is historical evidence of in-water performances in ancient Greece and Rome, as well as ancient Japan.

2. **Bullsh*t!** Men cannot compete in Olympic synchronized swimming competitions. Nor can they compete in World Championship competitions, although they are allowed to dip their toes into other international competitions.

3. **Fact.** Franklin was living proof that an athlete doesn't necessarily have to look like Atlas.

   He was posthumously inducted into the International Swimming Hall of Fame, and he penned his own tome on the art of swimming: *The Art of Swimming Rendered Easy: Directions to Learners, to Which Is Prefixed Advice to Bathers.*

KARATE!

1. Though karate is a Japanese martial art, it was invented by non-Japanese. It was first called *te*, but when it was later influenced by martial artists from China, it was called *kara te*, which translated to "Chinese hand."

2. In 2009, the International Olympic Committee (IOC) made karate an official Olympic sport. The only other Olympic martial art is judo.

3. While Chuck Norris won many karate championships, he has never been a karate fighter. Norris primarily studied a Korean martial art called tang soo do. Now Norris is the founder of his own martial art, chun kuk do, which is studied around the world.

1. **Fact.** A cultural exchange between China and Okinawa in the fourteenth century brought a whole settlement of Chinese families to the island. Practitioners of *te* began to exchange ideas and styles with practitioners of kung fu, and *kara te*, meaning "Chinese hand," was born. Okinawa was officially annexed by Japan in the nineteenth century.

   Today, the official Japanese translation for *karate* is "empty hand," since *karate* is a homophone that can mean both "Chinese hand" and "empty hand." It's likely they didn't like the fact that such a popular martial art was named after the Chinese.

   In Japan, the word is often elongated to *karate-dō*, which means "the way of the empty hand."

2. **Bullsh*t!** The IOC has considered karate for inclusion on multiple occasions, but **never approved it**. Beginning in 1964, judo was the only Olympic martial art, but it was joined by **tae kwon do** in 2000. The IOC is mum about their repeated denial of karate. A prominent theory is that the sport is too political, and that major karate organizations would not be able to agree on unified rules.

3. **Fact.** Chun kuk do was founded in 1990 by Norris and is based in Korean martial arts styles.

   Norris incorporates his personal philosophy into the teaching of chun kuk do, and students are exposed to his philosophical code, which includes "I will maintain an attitude of open-mindedness" and "I will always remain loyal to my God, my country, family, and my friends."

Fact. Fact. **Bullsh*t!**

THE JOCKSTRAP!

1. The word "jock," meaning athlete, is derived from "jockstrap." The "jock" in "jockstrap" is an abbreviation of "jockey." In the late nineteenth century, cyclists were called jockeys, and the jockstrap was invented for them.

2. In the early twentieth century, the Sears catalogue sold the Heidelberg Electric Belt, a jockstrap that delivered current to the genitals. The electricity was purported to "reduce anxiety" and solve a variety of other ailments.

3. In Middletown, Connecticut, the police department has been unsuccessful in its pursuit of the "Jockstrap Bandit." The unidentified man has committed an estimated seventeen armed robberies while wearing nothing but a mask, tennis shoes, and a jockstrap. Much to the chagrin of local authorities, the man has become a cult hero among area high school and university students.

1. **Fact.** Take heart in the fact that when you refer to an athlete as a "jock," you are in effect calling him a "jockstrap."

---

2. **Fact.** The Heidelberg belt was truly a marvel of science! It claimed to cure "weakness, exhaustion, impotency, rheumatism, sciatica, lame back, railroad back, insomnia, melancholia, kidney disorder, Bright's disease, dyspepsia, disorders of the liver, female weakness, poor circulation, weak heart action, and almost every known disease and weakness."

Considering all that it could do, it's a wonder that it's not still on the market.

3. **Bullsh*t!** That's a total fabrication.
It would lead to a pretty funny police lineup, however!

THE SPORTS BRA!

1. The first sports bra, invented in 1977 by Lisa Lindahl, was made from two jockstraps sewn together, and called the Jockbra. After a booming mail-order business, her company was purchased by Playtex.

2. A popular new sports bra on the market is the Wine Rack, which has a built-in bladder that you can fill with the beverage of your choice. A concealable rubber tube lets you sip away at the contents wherever you are. The makers insist that the Wine Rack can hold an entire bottle of wine, and argue that the bra is "better than a boob job, and cheaper too!"

3. Champion's Vapor sports bra incorporates a moisture-wicking fabric from an unlikely source: the cocoa tree. Structural fibers from the tree itself are woven into the fabric, prompting a popular nickname: "the chocolate bra."

1. **Fact.** According to Lindahl, her sister Victoria complained to her about soreness after jogging, and quipped, "Why isn't there a jockstrap for women?" Immediately, Lindahl's idea was born. She sewed together a bra out of two jockstraps, tested it out, and dubbed it the Jockbra.

   She later amended it to the Jogbra, since jogging was an enormous craze in the '70s. She did a landslide mail-order business and successfully marketed it to some stores. Eventually, Playtex bought the Jogbra company from Lindahl.

2. **Fact.** This is not a sports bra that you should wear while jogging.

   The company behind the product, Cooler Fun, also makes the Beer Belly—a refillable plastic beverage-holder that men can conceal under their shirts. The website suggests that you wear either product to "the movies, concerts, ball games, even PTA meetings."

3. **Bullsh*t!** The Vapor sports bra uses **Cocona fabric**, which is made from **coconuts**, and has several desirable qualities: evaporative cooling, odor absorption, and UV protection.

   Of course, if I told you women were beginning to exercise in coconut bras, you'd picture something else entirely.

THE CLEVELAND INDIANS!

1. The Cleveland Indians were established in 1901 as one of the first American League teams. The Indians have won the World Series twice, in 1920 and 1948. The Indians have gone the longest without a championship than any other team in the American League.

2. Cleveland Indians shortstop Ray Chapman was the only man in Major League Baseball history to be killed by a pitch.

3. In the late nineteenth century, Cleveland was home to three major league teams at once: the Cleveland Reds, the Cleveland Scorpions, and the Cleveland Billies.

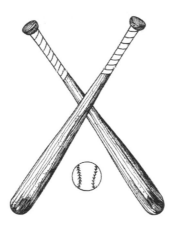

1. **Fact.** The only team to go longer is the Chicago Cubs of the National League, who haven't won a world series since 1908.

2. **Fact.** Chapman was struck in the head by a pitch from Yankee Carl Mays in an afternoon game on August 16, 1920. He died twelve hours later in the hospital.

   Mays' pitch was a spitball, and the Chapman incident led to the designation of the spitball as illegal.

3. **Bullsh*t!** It is true that even before the establishment of the American League and the Cleveland Indians in 1901, Cleveland was a major baseball city, and was home to multiple professional baseball teams. But, **Cleveland has never had three major league baseball teams at once.**

   Today, there are no Cleveland teams in the National League. But in the late nineteenth century, there were two: the **Cleveland Blues** (1879–1884) and the **Cleveland Spiders** (1887–1899). In 1890, a new league was formed called the Players' League, which only lasted for a year. The Cleveland team was called, believe it or not, the **Cleveland Infants**. Therefore, in 1890, Cleveland had two major league teams at once: the Spiders and the Infants. (The Players' League was not technically a major league at the time, but was declared one retroactively.)

Fact. Fact. **Bullsh*t!**

PING-PONG!

(a.k.a. table tennis)

1. Table tennis was first invented in Chicago in the 1850s. In those early days, the ball was made of tin, but when that proved too soft, it was replaced by a bronze alloy.

2. According to the International Table Tennis Federation, a regulation ball must be 2.7 grams in weight and 40 millimeters in diameter. The ball can only be white or orange, with a matte finish. Official competition balls are stored for three days at 73.4 degrees Fahrenheit, and then rigorously tested for bounce, veer, and hardness.

3. Unlike their finicky rules regarding the ball, the ITTF doesn't care what the table is made out of, as long as the ball bounces to a certain height when dropped on it.

1. **Bullsh*t!** The first "table tennis" patent was issued to David Foster in **England**, in **1890**. The sport had been played casually in England with improvised equipment during the decade before. Foster's version used a **cloth-covered rubber ball** and actual strung rackets!

2. **Fact.** The federation is very serious about ball suitability. There is an equipment committee, with a doctor in charge of it, and they use all kinds of electrical, computer, and machine equipment to test ping-pong balls.

3. **Fact.** The federation says that the playing surface can be made of any material as long as a ball (which meets their exacting standards) dropped from a height of 30 centimeters (not quite 12 inches) bounces about 23 centimeters (a little over 9 inches).

Fact. Fact. **Bullsh*t!**

WEIGHTLIFTING!

1. The word "dumbbell" comes from eighteenth-century England, when athletes would remove the clappers from church bells and exercise with them. The earliest-known versions of the dumbbell were rounded stones with handles called *halteres*, which were used for athletic training in ancient Greece.

2. The current all-time records for heaviest bench press and heaviest squat-lift both belong to Konstantynów Szczytniki, who lifted 1,350 pounds and 1,790 pounds in each category in 2010, beating previous records by more than a hundred pounds in both cases.

3. In 1990, hoping to capitalize on and repeat his success with the World Wrestling Federation, Vince McMahon launched the World Bodybuilding Federation. In the organization, bodybuilders (called BodyStars) were given colorful personalities and backstories similar to professional wrestlers.

1. **Fact.** A bell without its clapper would be mute, or "dumb" (which means mute but is now politically incorrect to use in the context of a person), hence the name "dumbbell." When actual dumbbells began to be made, the name stuck.

   The *halteres* began as weights to help long-jumpers train and eventually came to be used in the same manner as we use dumbbells today.

   At least 2,000 years ago, villagers in India began using club-shaped weights called *nals* for training.

2. **Bullsh*t!** No man walks the earth who is that great. Yet.

   Konstantynów and Szczytniki are both **places in Poland**.

   The all-time heaviest bench press record belongs to Ryan Kennelly, who lifted **1,075 pounds**, and the all-time heaviest squat-lift record belongs to Vladislav Alhazov, who lifted **1,250 pounds**, both in 2008.

3. **Fact.** Unfortunately, the WBF was a dismal failure and was disbanded in 1992.

PILLOW FIGHTING!

1. The Toronto-based Pillow Fight League is a semiprofessional sports league of scantily clad female competitors. Its regular events draw huge crowds and have been featured on national television. Popular fighters include Apocalipstick, Bobbi Pinn, and Olivia Neutron-Bomb.

---

2. On April 3, 2009, President Barack Obama and First Lady Michelle Obama posed in a mock pillow-fight photo op on the South Lawn of the White House. The first family armed themselves with pillows to be photographed with fourteen-year-old Holly Bingham-Greene, who was being honored for saving her father's life.

---

3. A 1905 *New York Times* headline read, "Ziegler Heir Recovers: Wealthy Boy Received His Injuries in a Pillow Fight."

1. **Fact.** The organization sprang up out of organized pillow-fighting nights at a goth club in Toronto. It has grown steadily and even recently sold television producing rights to its events. Official rules include "Female fighters only. No exceptions" and "Pillow fighters must practice good sportswomanship. No rude, lewd, or suggestive behavior."

2. **Bullsh*t!** There's not a single piece of truth in that statement at all. It's a total fabrication.

3. **Fact.** William Ziegler Jr. received his injuries playing with two schoolmates, and he recovered in "splendid condition," according to his physician.

STRANGE SPORTS!

1. A popular sport in Finland, wife carrying is now earning devotees in the United States. In the event, a man carries a woman through several hundred yards of an obstacle course to win a prize, often the wife's weight in beer. The most popular method employed is the Estonian carry, in which the woman hangs upside-down with her legs around the man's head.

---

2. The annual cheese-rolling competition in the Cotswolds region of England has been going on for more than two centuries. In the event, competitors chase a 7-to-8-pound double Gloucester cheese wheel down a steep hill. The person first to either catch it or cross the finish line wins the cheese after which they so valiantly chased.

---

3. Provided you're willing to travel, and perhaps risk life and limb, you could compete this year in any of the following sports: horizontal hurdles, baby-saving, kite-burping, cat lacrosse, lake checkers, face-wrestling, finger karate, and limousine-rolling.

1. Fact. The sport, called *eukonkanto* in Finland, is gaining popularity worldwide. These days, you can find major wife-carrying competitions in Finland, Estonia, India, Ireland, and the United States. The winner of the annual North American Wife Carrying Competition typically wins airfare for two to compete at the international championships in Finland.

Dennis Rodman attended the 2005 wife-carrying championship in Finland, but declined to participate because of health problems.

---

2. Fact. The event attracts hundreds of spectators and tourists a year. In theory, the competitors are attempting to catch the cheese, but with a one-second head start and rolling speeds as high as 70 miles per hour, nobody has ever caught an actively rolling cheese in the event. The competition happens at Cooper's Hill in Gloucester, a hill so steep that major injuries are common.

In the early '40s, thanks to food rationing, wooden cheese wheels were used, with tiny bits of cheese placed inside.

3. Bullsh*t! Those are all things I think **should** be sports.

But you **could compete in these**: the vertical marathon, coffin racing, nettle eating, dog surfing, swamp football, chess boxing, toe wrestling, and dead goat polo.

CHAPTER 7

Florilegium, Omnium-Gatherum, and Gallimaufry

"Florilegium," "omnium-gatherum," and "gallimaufry" are all, in essence, fancy ways of saying "miscellaneous stuff." It's like that junk drawer every house seems to have. When I was a kid, I would go to that drawer when I was bored. There was always something to entertain me, whether it was a comically oversized rubber band, a broken compass, or a bouncy ball with a chunk mysteriously missing. Of course, with my overactive imagination, I believed the contents of the drawer were truly miscellaneous: I half-expected to find a magic charm, a secret map, an Indian arrowhead, or a tiny alien. It would be nice to have a drawer with those capabilities, a drawer that, like this chapter, could be opened to reveal *anything*.

Can one be an expert at all things miscellaneous? Perhaps they should offer PhDs in miscellany—then you'd leave grad school prepared to be a doctor *or* a dominatrix. Or both. If you're an expert in miscellany, then you're really saying you're an expert in everything, and if you're an expert in everything, well, you should spot all the forthcoming bullshit with nary a problem at all.

Good luck!

THE TOOTHBRUSH!

1. The first mass-produced toothbrush was invented in 1780 in England. Before then, Europeans often used rags doused in soot and salt to clean their teeth. Sometimes the rag was attached to a stick to reach the back of the mouth.

2. In the nineteenth century, toothbrushes were often made of bone, and the bristles were actual animal hair. Horsehair, badger hair, and pig hair were all commonly used.

3. A toothbrush may seem like small potatoes when you throw it away, but environmental groups estimate 1 million pounds of plastic toothbrushes wind up in U.S. landfills in a given year. Laid end to end, that's enough toothbrushes to stretch from Chicago to Moscow.

1. **Fact.** To this day, there are people who advocate using soot as a (very abrasive) way to whiten teeth!

---

2. **Fact.** The most expensive bristles were made from badger hair, while horse and pig hair were also common. Synthetic bristles did not become standard until the 1940s.

3. **Bullsh*t!** Believe it or not, the actual estimate is **50 million** pounds of toothbrushes per year. While 10 million pounds of toothbrushes end to end would easily circumnavigate the globe, 50 million pounds is enough to **circle the planet five and three-quarters times**. Two years' worth of discarded toothbrushes, end to end, could reach the moon.

BANK ROBBERY!

1. In the U.S., a bank is robbed during business hours every twenty-five minutes. The perpetrators are caught, on average, between 40 and 50 percent of the time. The most popular time of day to rob a bank is during opening hours.

2. In 2008, a woman broke into a Somerset County, New Jersey, bank after closing. The police and a SWAT team surrounded the bank and engaged in a three-hour standoff with the woman, whom they could see silhouetted inside behind drawn shades. When the SWAT team finally broke in, they found a fully dressed mannequin. The woman had made her escape long before with over $8,000 in cash.

3. The biggest bank heist of all time was committed in 2003 at the Central Bank of Iraq, just hours before the U.S. bombing began. The robber, who made off with just under $1 billion, was none other than Qusay Hussein—Saddam's son.

1. **Fact.** The FBI keeps meticulous statistics on bank robberies. There are between 5,000 and 7,000 bank robberies each year, and the number seems to be slowly but steadily decreasing.

Each year, bank robbers make off with around $60 million.

2. **Bullsh*t!** That would make a good movie, though!

In truth, the police and the SWAT team **did engage in a three-hour standoff with a fake woman**, but she was a promotional cardboard cutout. The embarrassing incident did, in fact, end when the SWAT team broke in and found the cardboard lady and realized there had been **no break-in or theft** at all.

Police are still scratching their heads about what set off the alarm in the first place.

3. **Fact.** It took Qusay and his accomplices, as well as bank personnel, several hours to load the $950 million–plus into three trucks. Qusay bore a signed letter from his father himself, ordering the transaction, with the idea to keep the money out of American hands.

While the $650 million found inside the walls of one of Saddam's palaces is presumed to be part of the hoard, it has never been definitively linked to the bank. *None* of the stolen billion has been officially accounted for.

TOILET PAPER!

1. In the U.S., a household of four will, on average, use two trees' worth of toilet paper per year.

2. The first documented use of toilet paper in human history was in China in the sixth century A.D. By the ninth century A.D., using toilet paper was common in China (which is where paper was invented).

3. The inventor of modern commercially available toilet paper in the U.S. was an entrepreneur named Henry Joy. Joy's Therapeutic Paper was introduced in 1740, and was rolled up on thin wooden rods in packages of three.

1. **Fact.** The average American uses about 50 pounds of toilet and tissue paper per year. An average-sized tree will produce around 100 pounds of toilet paper. The math checks out.

   If every household in the U.S. traded out one roll of virgin toilet paper for recycled, we would, according to some experts, save 470,000 trees.

---

2. **Fact.** In 851 A.D., a traveler to China observed, "They [the Chinese] are not careful about cleanliness, and they do not wash themselves with water when they have done their necessities; but they only wipe themselves with paper."

   The ancient Egyptians were the first to use papyrus (around 3500 B.C.), but the Chinese were the first to make paper (105 A.D.). Papermaking did not become common practice in Europe until around 1400 A.D.

3. **Bullsh*t!** Commercially packed toilet paper in the U.S. did not arrive until **1857**, courtesy of **Joseph Gayetty**. It was called **Gayetty's Medicated Paper** and sold in **stacks of flat sheets**, each one watermarked with Gayetty's name.

   The first rolled paper was produced by the Scott Paper Company in 1879.

STONEHENGE!

1. Several of the monuments that comprise Stonehenge are tripetroids, or combinations of three stones, two standing upright, with a third lying flat on top of them. The fact they remain in place after thousands of years, with the stones lying loosely on top, is an architectural marvel.

---

2. A henge is a Neolithic piece of earthwork consisting of a man-made circular or oval-shaped bank, with a corresponding ditch running inside it. Stonehenge would be by far the world's most famous henge, except that its name is a misnomer: It is not a true henge at all.

---

3. In 1905, the Ancient Order of Druids held a massive ceremony at Stonehenge, initiating over 250 new members, much to the consternation of locals. The "druids" dressed the part: They wore long white robes and fake beards.

1. **Bullsh*t!** It may appear that each flat stone, or lintel, is just laying freely on top, but it is actually connected to the two uprights, or posts, with **complex jointing**. The lintels at Stonehenge are connected to the posts with mortise-and-tenon joints, which are basically knobs sticking up from the posts that fit into holes in the lintels. In the outer ring, the lintels are even joined, with tongue-and-groove joints.

   The freestanding structures of two posts and one lintel are called **trilithons**. "Tripetroids" is a totally made-up word.

2. **Fact.** Stonehenge does have a raised bank and a ditch, but the ditch runs outside of the bank, which means it is not actually a henge.

   Stone monuments are not required for something to be a henge, either. There are true henges with and without stones.

   It is totally silly that Stonehenge is not classified as a henge, because the word itself is derived from the name "Stonehenge."

3. **Fact.** The Ancient Order of Druids is a London fraternal organization that was founded in 1781 (not particularly ancient, after all) and still operates today. The society is an example of neo-druidism.

   The press ridiculed the 1905 gathering, particularly the costumes, and huge crowds of onlookers cheered and poked fun at the earnest disciples. Many locals were vexed by the unholy ceremony.

Fact. Fact. **Bullsh*t!**

VALENTINE'S DAY!

1. The Greeting Card Association estimates that 160 million valentines are sent each year. If you count children's packaged valentines, the number approaches 1 billion. Valentine's Day is the second-most-popular card-sending occasion in the United States, after Christmas.

2. In Saudi Arabia and Iran, Valentine's Day is the only Western holiday that it is legally permissible to celebrate. Conservative Islamic leaders forbid the practice of most Western-originated traditions, but make an exception for Valentine's Day based on the message. As Sheikh Ali Qarni of Saudi Arabia's Commission for Public Relations put it: "We join the world on this. We want to show that Muslims are people of love."

3. There were more than ten martyred saints named Valentine in ancient Rome. St. Valentine's Day could refer to as many as three of them. For this reason, Valentine's Day was removed in 1969 from the official Catholic calendar.

1. **Fact.** The figures are all courtesy of the Greeting Card Association, which also submitted this surprising factoid: The most popular colors for Valentines are red and pink. Amazing! I was sure they'd be camouflage and tin foil.

2. **Bullsh*t!** In Saudi Arabia and Iran, celebrating Valentine's Day is **outlawed**. In Saudi Arabia, shopkeepers are ordered to **destroy any cards, roses, candy, and teddy bears** in their inventory, as well as **anything red**, or face reprisal from **religious police**.

   However, the holiday is **popular anyway** in both places; citizens celebrate unobtrusively or in full-fledged secrecy.

   Sheikh Ali Qarni of Saudi Arabia's **Commission for Promotion of Virtue and Prevention of Vice** (you can't make this stuff up) defended the ban, pointing out that Muslims embrace the true meaning of love, which is the love of God. "Muslims are people of love, as evidenced by the fact that this word appears in [the Koran] eighty-three times," he said.

3. **Fact.** Of the three Valentines that could be the source of the name "Valentine's Day," none were associated with love or romance. Popular legend sometimes recounts the story of an imprisoned St. Valentine sending one last romantic note to his beloved, but the story has no basis in historical fact.

   All three saints in question were martyrs, however, and early religious observances of the holiday focused on martyrdom rather than love and romance. The Catholic Church removed the holiday from the calendar in 1969 because of the lack of data about St. Valentine.

Fact. Fact. **Bullsh*t!**

NEW JERSEY!

1. Most of New Jersey lies within the New York and Philadelphia metropolitan areas, and as of 2011 it is the most densely populated U.S. state (and has been for decades).

2. About 250 million years ago, the land that is now New Jersey was immediately adjacent to the land that is now the western Sahara Desert, in Africa. New Jersey still contains rocks from the African plate.

3. The New Jersey state bird is the ruffed grouse, its state dance is the polka, the state animal is the white-tailed deer, and the official state song is "I'm From New Jersey."

1. Fact. The District of Columbia is much more densely populated than New Jersey, but it is not a state, so it doesn't qualify. As of the 2010 census count, with nearly 1,200 people per square mile, the Garden State is definitely the most densely populated.

A metropolitan area is a major urban region linked socially and economically. Even though New York City is unquestionably in New York State, twelve New Jersey counties are part of the New York metropolitan area and five are in the Philadelphia metropolitan area (an additional three are on the fence). There are twenty-one counties in New Jersey.

---

2. Fact. Geologists have proven that some 250 million years ago, during the Paleozoic and Mesozoic eras, all of the earth's continents were joined into one supercontinent, often called Pangaea. Rifts formed, and the continent split into the several continents we recognize on maps today. Our continents are still moving.

When Africa and New Jersey split, chunks of the African plate remained fused to New Jersey. When you stand on the New Jersey coast, you are standing on top of rocks that were once part of Africa.

3. Bullsh*t! The ruffed grouse, the polka, and the white-tailed deer are the state bird, dance, and animal of **Pennsylvania**.

New Jersey is the **only state** that does not have a state song. Some people consider "I'm From New Jersey" to be the state song, but officially, it is not.

SEVERED FEET!

1. A family dog from Russellville, Alabama, made national headlines in 2008 for bringing home the severed foot of a child. Police went into high alert, searching surrounding areas with cadaver-sniffing dogs and consulting numerous missing-child databases. The hysteria immediately ceased a couple of days later when forensic tests results showed that the foot was actually a bear paw.

2. Between August 2007 and December 2010, detached human feet have been discovered along the coastline of Washington State and British Columbia on ten separate occasions. The majority of feet discovered were wearing socks and tennis shoes.

3. The foot of a nine-year-old Chinese girl named Ming Li was severed in July of 2010, when she was run over by a tractor on her way to school. Surgeons found the foot to be too damaged to reattach straightaway, so they grafted it to her other leg to let it heal. An entire month later, they successfully reattached her foot to its proper place.

1. **Fact.** Police Chief Chris Hargett hastened to point out that the paw resembled a foot closely enough that it fooled an orthopedic surgeon.

---

2. **Fact.** The first foot, discovered on August 20, 2007, was a right male foot in a Campus shoe. The second foot, found on August 26, 2007, was a right male foot in a Reebok. The third foot, found on February 8, 2008, was a right male foot in a Nike. The fourth foot, found on May 22, 2008, was a right female foot in a New Balance. The fifth foot, found on June 16, 2008, was a left male foot that was DNA-matched with the third foot. The sixth foot, found on August 1, 2008, was a right male foot in an Everest shoe. The seventh foot, found on November 11, 2008, was a left female foot that was DNA-matched with the fourth foot. The eighth foot, found on October 27, 2009, was a bare right male foot. The ninth foot, found on August 27, 2010, was a bare right foot belonging to a woman or a child. The tenth foot, found on December 5, 2010, was a right male foot in a hiking boot.

   Something is definitely afoot.

3. **Bullsh*t!** The story is close to the truth, but the reality is **even cooler**. Ming Li lost not her foot, but her **hand** in the accident. The left hand was **grafted to her right calf** while it healed, and it was successfully reattached to her wrist **three months** later.

Fact. Fact. **Bullsh*t!**

THE WHITE HOUSE!

1. African-American slaves helped to build the White House. President John Adams, the first to move into the White House, was against the practice of slavery, so his staff contained no slaves.

2. The White House has a tennis court, a putting green, a billiards room, a jogging track, a swimming pool, and a bowling alley, thanks to Presidents Theodore Roosevelt, Dwight Eisenhower, John Quincy Adams, Bill Clinton, Gerald Ford, and Richard Nixon, respectively.

3. The White House has exactly eighty-eight rooms on four levels, including sixteen bathrooms. There are 198 doors, 100 windows, six fireplaces, three staircases, and an elevator. The original walls of the White House were built out of white limestone (that's how it got its name), and it takes 280 gallons of paint to cover its outside surface.

1. **Fact.** The workers themselves represent a slice of American cultural history. Many were slaves, many were immigrants, and some were free African Americans. Our second president, John Adams, was the first to live in the White House, and he never owned a slave.

---

2. **Fact.** Teddy Roosevelt had tennis courts built behind the West Wing in 1902.

   Eisenhower had the first putting green installed outside the Oval Office.

   John Quincy Adams put the first billiards table in the White House in 1825, but certainly not the last.

   Clinton had a jogging track built around the south grounds during his first term.

   Gerald Ford built an outdoor swimming pool on the South Lawn in 1975.

   President Nixon was an avid bowler, and friends had a one-lane alley built for him in a White House basement room in 1969–1970. The alley remains!

3. **Bullsh*t!** In the White House, there are **132 rooms on six levels**, including **thirty-five bathrooms**. There are **412 doors, 147 windows, twenty-eight fireplaces, eight staircases,** and **three elevators**.

   The original walls of the White House were built out of **gray sandstone**, and they are still in place. "The White House" became a nickname for the house in the early nineteenth century when it was painted white, and it became the official name after Theodore Roosevelt proclaimed it so in 1901.

   It takes **570** gallons of paint to cover the White House's surface.

HOLY COW!!!

1. The phrase "holy cow!" started to find common usage in the 1930s, but was popularized by baseball announcers in the decades after—particularly in the '50s and '60s by broadcasting legend Phil Rizzuto, who used the phrase prodigiously. When the former Yankee shortstop's number was retired in a 1985 ceremony, an actual cow wearing a halo was brought onstage.

2. In many Hindu traditions the cow is regarded as holy Cows are seen as symbols of sacrifice, wealth, and strength. The 1,500-year-old *Mahabharata* says, "Cows are the foremost of all things . . . there is nothing more sacred or sanctifying than cows."

3. If you look closely at the chandelier hanging in the middle of the Massachusetts Senate chamber, you'll notice that a brass casting of a cow is incorporated into it. The casting is fondly nicknamed "the Holy Cow," and also has a counterpart in the House of Representatives chamber in the Massachusetts State House, in the form of a painted cow portrait. The painting was famously stolen in 1933 by members of the *Harvard Lampoon* in an incident called the "Cow-Napping."

1. **Fact.** Rizzuto's exclamations of "holy cow!" punctuated many dramatic moments in Yankee history, and led to multiple cow-themed tributes to the man. At the 1985 ceremony, the live "holy" cow accidentally (and comically) knocked Rizzuto off his feet.

2. **Fact.** In traditional Hindu societies, even the vegetarians derive a lot of benefit from cows. Milk, curds, and ghee (clarified butter) provide the basis for their diet. Cows perform labor by pulling carts and plows. Even cow dung has its uses: It is an excellent fuel when burned, and because it contains ammonia and menthol, burning dung repels mosquitoes and even acts as a disinfectant. That cows provide all these things is seen as the embodiment of merit.

3. **Bullsh*t!** There is no cow in that chandelier, and there was no "cow-napping."

   However, there is incorporated into the chandelier in the Massachusetts Senate chamber **a brass casting of a fish**, which is colloquially known as the **Holy Mackerel**. It's believed to be the counterpart to the **Sacred Cod**, a 1784 carving of a codfish that hangs in the House of Representatives chamber.

   The Sacred Cod was famously pilfered in 1933 by members of the *Harvard Lampoon* in an incident known as the "**Cod-Napping**." It was returned two days later after members of the House **refused to legislate without the cod present**.

1950!

1. In 1950, President Truman ended racial segregation in the military, Israel declared its independence, and the Republic of Korea was established.

2. In 1950, *South Pacific* won the Pulitzer Prize for Drama and the Tony Award for Best Musical. The Academy Award for Best Picture went to *All the King's Men*. The first *Peanuts* and *Beetle Bailey* comic strips appeared in newspapers.

3. In 1950 the United States population was 152,271,417. The average household income was $4,237. There were slightly more women than men, but they only made up 28.8 percent of the workforce.

1. **Bullsh*t!** All of those things happened in **1948**.

2. **Fact.** In 1950, we also saw the first kidney transplant and the first TV remote control (it was connected to a wire). The Yankees won the World Series, and the NBA championship went to the Minneapolis Lakers.

3. **Fact.** The United States population has more than doubled since 1950, and we now make ten times as much money on average, although adjusting for inflation, we make about one and a half times as much money. These days, there are still more women than men, and they make up a little less than half of the workforce.

HUGS!

1. A 2010 study by animal behaviorists at the DuPage Animal Hospital in Villa Park, Illinois, proved that dogs that are "routinely held, hugged, and cuddled with" are three times as likely to live longer and remain healthier than dogs that aren't. The study inspired the Humane Society to distribute bumper stickers that say "Have you hugged your dog today?"

2. In a major new national trend, schools across the country have been instituting a new ban in hopes to keep our kids safe. The dangerous culprit from which we need to protect them? Hugs.

3. A study at the University of North Carolina concluded that hugging can lower your blood pressure. Interestingly, the effect was much more pronounced on women than men.

1. Bullsh*t! Nothing true in that paragraph.

In fact, animal behaviorists assert that **dogs don't like to be hugged**, even when it's their beloved master doing the embracing. When dogs place a limb over or around another dog, or superimpose their bodies over another, it is a **sign of dominance and aggression**.

The scientists go on to say that hugging a dog you're not familiar with is a good way to **get bitten**.

So, next time you want to show Spot that you love him, lick his face instead.

2. Fact. The hug threat is being addressed at our schools with varying levels of severity, from outright bans on any form of physical contact (even the high-five), to strict time limits of two or three seconds per hug.

Didn't you hear? Hugs are the new drugs.

---

3. Fact. The North Carolina study is just one of a multitude that show loving physical contact is demonstrably beneficial to health. In the study, the huggers showed decreased blood pressure for long after the actual hug, and even during the recounting of a stressful memory.

Both men and women also showed increased levels of oxytocin, sometimes called the "love hormone," which is supposed to have a beneficial effect on the heart.

The dip in blood pressure was more pronounced in women, and women also showed a clear dip in cortisol, which is known as the "stress hormone."

I think the next logical step would be for our president to pass a law providing universal hug care for all Americans.

IMPOSTORS!

1. Joshua Abraham Norton was a British-born businessman and resident of San Francisco who, on September 17, 1859, declared himself emperor of the United States. During his "reign," the "Imperial Majesty of these United States" issued numerous decrees, ate at any San Francisco restaurant for free, issued his own currency (which was accepted anywhere in the city), and declared himself "Protector of Mexico."

---

2. In the late '90s, the Paul VI Catholic High School in Fairfax, Virginia, was delighted to welcome sixteen-year-old incoming student Jonathan Taylor Spielberg, the rich nephew of director Steven Spielberg. Not long into his tenure at the high school, it was revealed that "Spielberg" was actually Anoushirvan Fakhun, a twenty-seven-year-old former porn actor from Iran.

---

3. In the 1970s, Dr. Charlotte Bach taught biology at the University of East London for three years before it was revealed that she had never been a scientist, and, in fact, had never even earned a college degree.

1. **Fact.** The emperor was so beloved by locals that his seal of approval led to increased business for merchants (hence his free meal ticket at any restaurant) and his self-issued currency was collectible and valuable (and therefore accepted tender in San Francisco).

   When a local police officer arrested Norton in hopes of committing him to an asylum, locals responded with outrage. Norton was released, the police apologized, and, from then on, he was routinely saluted in the streets by the boys in blue.

   Norton ordered the construction of both a bridge and a tunnel across San Francisco Bay. Like all of his decrees, it was ignored, but the Transbay Tube (built in 1969) bears a plaque of "Norton I, Emperor of the United States, Protector of Mexico" to this day.

---

2. **Fact.** When his fakery was found out, Fakhran received an eleven-month suspended sentence and a hundred hours of community service. When asked why he did it, he said, "Just for the fun, to get the experience I never had."

3. **Bullsh*t!** Dr. Charlotte Bach never taught at the University of East London. She was a **fringe evolutionary theorist** with a large following among scientists and intellectuals in 1970s London and **thought to be a former lecturer at Budapest's Eötvös Loránd University**. Upon her death in 1981, it was revealed that Dr. Charlotte Bach was **never a scientist or a professor**, and indeed was **never Dr. Charlotte Bach**: She was actually **Karoly Hajdu**, a **Hungarian immigrant**, **former criminal**, and most shockingly, **a man**.

RARE BOOKS!

1. The most expensive printed book ever sold was a copy of John Audubon's *Birds of America*, which was purchased at auction in 2010 for $11.5 million. The most expensive manuscript ever sold was Leonardo da Vinci's handwritten *Codex Leicester*, which Bill Gates bought in 1994 for $30.8 million.

2. The libraries of both Brown and Harvard universities contain books bound in human skin.

3. The Voynich manuscript, a handwritten book on 240 vellum pages from the early fifteenth century, and containing essays on natural history, religion, astronomy, mysticism, and mathematics, is believed to have been written by Matthias Voynich, who was seven years old at the time.

1. **Fact.** Only 119 copies of Audobon's *Birds of America* are thought to exist, eleven of which are in private hands.

   The *Codex Leicester* contains seventy-two pages of Leonardo da Vinci's personal scientific writings and drawings. Gates scanned the document and included the images as a screen saver in Windows 95.

   Nice of him to share.

---

2. **Fact.** The practice of binding books in human skin was commonplace at a couple of times in human history, and is known as anthropodermic bibliopegy. Several such tomes still exist today in rare book collections, including the copy of *Practicarum quaestionum circa leges regias Hispaniae* in Harvard's law library that bears this inscription: "The bynding of this booke is all that remains of my deare friende Jonas Wright, who was flayed alive."

   Creepy.

3. **Bullsh*t!** The Voynich manuscript **is** a handwritten book on 240 vellum pages from the early fifteenth century. As far as we know, the book was **not** written by a seven-year-old, or anyone named Matthias. All 35,000 words are written in **an unknown language** with **an unknown alphabet**, and, since its discovery in 1912, **nobody has been able to translate or decode it**, including celebrated cryptographers, military code breakers, and sophisticated computers. The book is genuinely from the early fifteenth century, and its language does follow normal patterns of the written word (and is therefore not gibberish), but the meaning of those words is still lost on us today.

PAJAMAS!

1. The word "pajama" is originally derived from the Persian word *paejamah*, which means "leg clothing." The word was adopted by the British during their presence in India in the eighteenth and nineteenth centuries.

2. According to a recent ABC News poll, only 10 percent of Americans wear pajamas to bed. Some 33 percent responded that they wear underwear to bed, and a whopping 48 percent responded that they *wear nothing at all*.

3. A Welsh supermarket caused an international stir when it instituted a strict no-pajamas policy in 2010. Customers in PJs were turned away at the door.

1. Fact. The Indian version in the nineteenth century was *pai jamahs*, which were actually loose-fitting pants. The British found them exceedingly comfortable, and brought them home. Eventually, they became common sleepwear.

"Pajama" is sometimes spelled "pyjama," which is the primary spelling in England and Canada.

2. Bullsh*t! You wanted to believe it, though, right?

The survey showed that 33 percent of Americans wear pajamas to bed, 23 percent wear "shorts/ T-shirt," 16 percent wear underwear, 22 percent go naked, and 1 percent wear "sweatshirt/sweatpants." In the poll, 2 percent responded that they wear "something else," which I assume includes such popular choices as astronaut suit, scuba gear, diaper, and chain mail.

3. Fact. The Tesco supermarket in Cardiff posted this rule "To avoid causing offence or embarrassment to others we ask that our customers are appropriately dressed when visiting our store (footwear must be worn at all times and no nightwear is permitted)." BBC News interviewed at least one customer who was turned away: a full-time mother of two who was swinging by the store after dropping her kids off. Her reaction? "I think it's stupid."

The dress code ignited debates in both the U.K. and the U.S. about the habit of wearing sleepwear in public, and whether it should be regulated or not.

I say let it go. If you ban pajamas today, you might ban pirate costumes tomorrow, and none of us want that, do we?

ELEVEN!

1. Eleven is an extremely significant number in multiple religions: In Hinduism, a feast is organized on the eleventh day of death. Eleven is the number of nodes in Metatron's Cube, which is used in the Kabbalah. Eleven is the traditional number of witches in a Wiccan coven. According to the Torah, God has eleven attributes of mercy.

---

2. The word "eleven" comes from the German word meaning "one left over," because it's the first number that can't be counted using the fingers (and thumbs) of both hands.

---

3. The armistice with Germany, which ended World War I, occurred on the eleventh hour of the eleventh day of the eleventh month of the year.

1. **Bullsh*t!** All of these statements are true of the number thirteen, not eleven.

2. **Fact.** The Old High German word is *einlif*, literally meaning "one remaining." The Old English word, meaning essentially the same thing, is *endeleofan*. In case you were wondering.

---

3. **Fact.** The agreement between the Allies and Germany was made at 5 A.M. on November 11, 1918, but was set to go into effect at 11 A.M. The last six hours were marked by a surge in fighting, as many wanted to get in the last best shot before the cease-fire.

    Armistice Day is still celebrated on November 11.

MURDER!

1. According to the FBI, there were 28,138 murders in the United States in 2009. Of this number, just over 16,000 were committed with firearms. Forty-eight cases were murder by poison, and there were twenty-seven murders by *explosives.*

---

2. "If a man commits murder, that man must be killed" was written in the Sumerian Code of Ur-Nammu at around 2050 B.C., making it the oldest known codified law against murder.

---

3. In 2006, a German man, Armin Meiwes, was convicted of the 2001 murder of Bernd Jürgen Brandes. The case was controversial because Brandes *consented* beforehand to the murder, and furthermore, *requested to be eaten* by Meiwes

1. **Bullsh*t!** Things aren't nearly that bad. A truly accurate number is hard to come by, but the FBI estimates around **13,636** reported murders for 2009, with **9,146** by firearms. There were **six** murders by poison, and **two** by explosives.

2. **Fact.** The Code of Ur-Nammu is the oldest-known example of a written code of law that survives today. It is attributed to the king of Ur at the time, Ur-Nammu.

---

3. **Fact.** Meiwes posted an online ad, looking for victims to be slaughtered and eaten. Brandes eagerly answered the ad and stated that it was his wish to be killed and consumed.

Brandes went to Meiwes's house, where Meiwes videotaped the murder and butchering of the body. He proceeded to freeze most of it and consume the flesh over the course of several months.

Meiwes is known as the "Cannibal of Rotenburg."

TUESDAY!

1. In English, Tuesday gets its name from a one-handed god of war in Norse mythology. In most Romance languages, Tuesday is named after the Roman god of war.

2. Fat Tuesday has been observed annually in New Orleans since its founding as the capital of French Louisiana in 1702, making it the oldest Fat Tuesday celebration in America.

3. Keith Richards wrote the Rolling Stones song "Ruby Tuesday" about a groupie named Linda Keith, who quit following the band and later became involved with Jimi Hendrix. The Ruby Tuesday restaurant chain is named after the song.

1. **Fact.** "Tuesday" comes from "Tiw's Day," and *Tiw* is the Old English version of the Norse *Týr*. Týr was a warrior from the Nordic pantheon, who was associated with combat, tactics, law, and victory. The legend says that Týr sacrificed his hand to the great wolf Fenrir.

   Mars was the Roman god of war, and is often identified as an analogue of Týr. "Tiw's Day" may have been a translation of the Latin *dies Martis*, or "Day of Mars." Tuesday in most Romance languages is named after *Martis*, such as the French *mardi*, Spanish *martes*, Italian *martedi*, Catalan *dimarts*, and Romanian *marți*. Even the Irish use it: *Dé Máirt*.

   Other languages prefer Týr over Mars, as English does, such as the Danish *tirsdag*, Swedish *tisdag*, and Finnish *tiistai*.

   In either case, Tuesday is a good day to do battle. Tell that to your coworkers.

2. **Bullsh*t!** New Orleans wasn't founded until **1718**. **Mobile** was founded as the capital of French Louisiana in 1702, even though it is now, of course, firmly in Alabama. Mobile's original Fat Tuesday (which translated into French is *mardi gras*) celebrations were the first in America, and continue to this day.

3. **Fact.** Keith Richards said the song was "about Linda Keith not being there. She had pissed off somewhere. It was very mournful . . . and it was a Tuesday."

   The first Ruby Tuesday restaurant was founded in 1972, five years after "Ruby Tuesday" was released and hit number one on the music charts.

PINK!

1. We call our little fingers "pinkies" because, with young children, the little finger is often the rosiest.

---

2. Before the 1930s, it was commonly held in the United States that blue was for girls and pink was for boys.

---

3. In the seventeenth century, if you sent your sheets to be dyed pink, you'd be very likely to get them back bearing a rich shade of yellow.

1. Bullsh*t! We get the word "pinky" (or "pinkie") from the Dutch word *pink*, which means . . . wait for it . . . "little finger."

2. Fact. Pink, as a shade of red, was thought to be a bolder color, more suitable for masculinity. Blue, which is associated with the Virgin Mary, was thought to be soft and feminine.

In a 1918 issue of *Ladies' Home Journal*, you can find this passage: "The generally accepted rule is pink for the boy and blue for the girl. The reason is that pink being a more decided and stronger colour is more suitable for the boy, while blue, which is more delicate and dainty, is prettier for the girl."

---

3. Fact. Back then, "pink" or "pinke" referred to the pigment extracted from unripe buckthorn berries, which was similar in shade to goldenrod yellow. The pigment is now called "stil de grain yellow." "Pink" did not become the widespread word for the cotton-candy color we know and love until the eighteenth century.

Fact. Fact. **Bullsh*t!**

THE PENCIL!

1. The world's largest pencil is 76 feet long, weighs 22,000 pounds, and contains 4,000 pounds of Pennsylvania graphite. It was built by Ashrita Furman, who has set more than three hundred Guinness World Records in his lifetime.

---

2. Though he's remembered primarily as a philosopher, Henry David Thoreau was also an inventor, and he often included the words "civil engineer" after his name. His father was a pencil maker, and Thoreau was an avid participant in the business, designing a pencil-making technique that turned the business into a wild success.

---

3. Ernest Hemingway and Jack Kerouac were avid pencil pushers, using the implement to write their books. Hemingway sometimes went through sixty pencils in one day. Cormac McCarthy writes all his books exclusively in pencil.

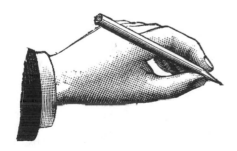

1. **Fact.** One of Furman's records is for "the most current Guinness world records held at the same time by an individual."

   Furman's records are eclectic, such as the "fastest mile on a kangaroo ball," a record that he set while on the Great Wall of China.

   Furman's enormous pencil cost $20,000 to produce and beat the 65-foot pencil that sits outside of pencil maker Faber-Castell's headquarters in Malaysia.

---

2. **Fact.** Thoreau spent a lot of his adult life pitching in to the family business. He discovered a way to mix inferior graphite with clay to make a smooth-writing pencil of any hardness desired. The result was a booming pencil company.

   Of course, Thoreau being Thoreau, he walked away from the success and sought no personal gain from the invention.

3. **Bullsh*t!** Hemingway and Kerouac favored **the typewriter**, as does McCarthy, who may be the most famous surviving writer to still use the machine exclusively. In 2009, McCarthy's typewriter, on which he believes he wrote 5 million words, sold at auction for $254,500.

   John Steinbeck was a pencil fanatic, sometimes going through sixty pencils in one day. It is said that he would start each writing day with twenty-four sharpened pencils, which he would need to re-sharpen before the day was out. He spent 300 pencils in the writing of *East of Eden*.

Fact. Fact. **Bullsh*t!**

FELINE CRUELTY!

1. In a top-secret 1967 experiment, the CIA surgically implanted a set of microphones and a battery into a cat, and an antenna in its tail, hoping to use the poor animal for spy missions. In its first test mission, operatives directed the cat to eavesdrop on a pair of men outside of the Soviet compound in Washington, D.C. As soon as the cat was released, it darted into the street and was promptly run over and killed by a taxi cab. The project was scrapped.

2. In late medieval France, a truly disgusting spectacle was common during midsummer festivals: cat burning. Dozens of live cats would be collected in a bag or net and suspended over a bonfire. Revelers collected the ashes afterward, believing them to be good luck.

3. In the 1940 Soviet "science" film *Experiments in the Revival of Organisms*, the severed head of a cat is shown to be kept alive by receiving a steady supply of oxygenated blood from an artificial heart and lung simulator called an autojector. The head responds to stimuli such as being poked and being brushed with a feather.

1. **Fact.** The operation was nicknamed by the people involved "Acoustic Kitty." Despite the $15 million price tag, the dead prototype, and the discontinuation of the project, the CIA memo reported that the experiment was a "remarkable scientific achievement" because "cats can indeed be trained to move short distances."

---

2. **Fact.** It's horrible, deplorable, and awful, but it's true. In 1648, King Louis XIV lit the fire himself.

   In many medieval societies, animals were believed to represent different sides of human nature (look up "scapegoat"), and cats had the awful luck of being associated with the evils in humanity and the devil. For that reason, burning cats was not regarded as cruel; instead it was seen as a way to cleanse society of evil.

   How doing something evil can cleanse evil, don't ask me!

3. **Bullsh*t!** Is the story true? No. Is it far-fetched? No. In fact, the whole thing happened as I described it, except it was the **head of a dog**, not a cat.

   To this day, the scientific community doesn't know what to make of the movie. Some believe it is real and have even cited the experiments in articles and papers, and some believe it was a hoax video, made for the purposes of Soviet propaganda.

   Either way, it's very, very disturbing.

EXPLODING WHALES!

1. In 1970, an 8-ton sperm whale beached itself on the Oregon coast and promptly died. Cleanup fell under the jurisdiction of the Oregon Highway Division, which decided the most logical course of action was to blow it up. A thousand pounds of dynamite were strapped to the carcass and detonated.

---

2. In 2004, a 56-foot-long, 60-ton sperm whale beached itself on the Taiwan coast and promptly died. It took three cranes and fifty workers thirteen hours to get the carcass on the back of an eighteen-wheeler so that it could be transported to a wildlife study center. En route, in the urban center of the bustling city of Tainan, the whale exploded, showering shops, cars, and onlookers with blood and rotting entrails.

---

3. In 2010, a 30-foot-long humpback whale became stranded in shallow water near the Western Australia coast, prompting authorities to attempt to tow it back to safety. Before the rescue mission was underway, the whale spontaneously exploded. Nobody was injured, as the whale was safely underwater, and the carcass was towed out to sea anyway. Scientists, unable to examine the body, have offered no adequate explanation for the bizarre bursting.

1. **Fact.** The theory went that the dynamite would effectively disintegrate the massive carcass, leaving pieces small enough for scavengers to clean up.

   Immediately after the explosion it became apparent that the technique was not beneficial. Large pieces of whale and globs of blubber rained down on buildings and parking lots some distance away, causing damage. As for the whale—only part of it was disintegrated, leaving a massive smoking whale pile for the Oregon Highway Division to clean up.

2. **Fact.** The explosion was caused by a natural buildup of gas inside the decomposing whale. A crowd of more than 600 had gathered in the street to watch the bizarre procession, only to have their day go horribly wrong.

   No matter how bad a day you're having, remember, it could be worse!

3. **Bullsh*t!** In 2010, a 30-foot-long humpback whale **did** become stranded in shallow water near the Western Australia coast, and it **did explode**, though not naturally. Authorities decided to **euthanize** the trapped animal by blowing it up. They succeeded.

Fact. Fact. **Bullsh*t!**

LAUGHTER!

1. Chimpanzees, bonobos, gorillas, orangutans, dogs, and rats all laugh.

---

2. On average, children laugh at least ten times as often as adults on a daily basis. Laughter can lower your blood pressure, reduce pain, increase vascular blood flow, and improve your ability to learn.

---

3. I laughed out loud 357 times and cried once while writing this book.

1. **Fact.** So do humans!

    Ape laughter sounds quite different from ours (like a combination between breathing and shrieking), but it is definitely present in both captive and wild apes during tickling and horseplay.

    Dog laughter sounds to us like heavy panting, but the pattern is quite different from what you'd hear from an out-of-breath dog. Dogs laugh when they play, and research has proven that the sound of a dog laughing elicits a play response in other nearby dogs.

    Scientists have proven that rats are ticklish, and while being tickled or engaged in rough-and-tumble play they emit ultrasonic vocalization patterns that seem to be primitive laughter.

---

2. **Fact.** Multiple studies have consistently proven that laughter provides a whole host of health benefits. They should call comedians doctors.

    Not to put a damper on things, but I'd be remiss if I didn't point out that laughter can also kill. Laughter can cause atony (muscle failure), which can lead to syncope (fainting), which in turn can put you in jeopardy. In one reported case, a Danish man died during a laughing fit while watching *A Fish Called Wanda*.

    Still, I think it's worth the risk.

3. **Bullsh*t!** According to my estimates, I laughed nearly 10,000 times and cried twice. When things are so strange that the truth sounds like lies, it's obvious we live in a fascinating world!

    I hope you had half as much fun reading this book as I had writing it, because I've had a ball.

ABOUT THE AUTHOR

Neil Patrick Stewart is a writer, teacher, director, actor, and a devoted spermologist. He loves variety above all things: He has been a food-and-beverage writer for major magazines; he's coached middle-school girls' volleyball; he's toured France three times performing Shakespeare; he's taught thousands of young actors in special workshops and at the legendary Broadway Theatre Project; he's driven across the country fourteen times; he's danced in two seasons of the Fort Worth Ballet's productions of *The Nutcracker* and *Cinderella*; he's lived in Russia; he's interviewed celebrities; he's filmed a movie in the Egyptian desert; and he's worked as a professional chef, a literary expert, a fact-checker, a tutor, a mover, a ticket-taker, a babysitter, a speech coach, a life coach, a cashier, a deejay, an event planner, a book-seller, a proofreader, a personal assistant, a voice-over actor, a police decoy, a builder, a driver, and a pizza-slicer. With this book, he adds author to the list.

Neil thanks the Stewart and Raymund families for their encouragement, his friends for their suggestions, the cast of *Julius Caesar* for putting up with his trivia obsession, his mother and sister for their proofreading skills, his friend Juliet for helping him realize that he's a writer, Jennifer and Brendan from Adams Media for above-and-beyond support, and, most of all, his gorgeous wife Monica, the love of his life, for inspiring him (and making him lunch) every day as he wrote this book.

Visit *www.neilpatrickstewart.com* and follow Neil on Twitter (@bald).

DAILY BENDER

Want Some More?

Hit up our humor blog, The Daily Bender, to get your fill of all things funny—be it subversive, odd, offbeat, or just plain mean. The Bender editors are there to get you through the day and on your way to happy hour. Whether we're linking to the latest video that made us laugh or calling out (or bullshit on) whatever's happening, we've got what you need for a good laugh.

If you like our book, you'll love our blog. (And if you hated it, "man up" and tell us why.) Visit The Daily Bender for a shot of humor that'll serve you until the bartender can.

Sign up for our newsletter at

www.adamsmedia.com/blog/humor

and download our Top Ten Maxims No Man Should Live Without.